50 French Cake Flavor Recipes for Home

By: Kelly Johnson

Table of Contents

- Tarte Tatin
- Madeleines
- Financiers
- Opéra Cake
- Clafoutis
- Gâteau Basque
- Paris-Brest
- Charlotte aux Fraises
- Gâteau au Yaourt
- Mille-feuille
- Gâteau Saint-Honoré
- Tarte au Citron
- Baba au Rhum
- Pithiviers
- Galette des Rois
- Choux à la Crème
- Gâteau de Mamie
- Tarte aux Pommes
- Gâteau au Chocolat
- Tarte Bourdaloue
- Tarte aux Framboises
- Gâteau Mont-Blanc
- Crêpes Suzette
- Tarte au Chocolat
- Tarte à la Praliné
- Gâteau au Miel
- Tarte à l'Orange
- Gâteau de Crêpes
- Gâteau au Fromage Blanc
- Tarte aux Poireaux
- Tarte aux Pêches
- Gâteau au Praliné
- Madeleines au Citron
- Tarte aux Noix
- Cannelés
- Tarte au Fromage

- Gâteau à la Vanille
- Tarte aux Mûres
- Tarte au Caramel
- Gâteau au Café
- Tarte au Pralin
- Tarte au Chocolat et aux Noix
- Tarte au Crumble
- Gâteau au Pêches et au Miel
- Tarte aux Amandes
- Tarte aux Abricots
- Gâteau de Voyage
- Gâteau à la Crème de Marron
- Tarte aux Raisins
- Tarte au Miel et aux Amandes

Tarte Tatin

Ingredients:

- **For the Caramel:**
    - 1 cup (200g) granulated sugar
    - 1/4 cup (60g) unsalted butter
- **For the Apples:**
    - 6 to 8 medium-sized apples (such as Granny Smith or Braeburn)
    - 1 tablespoon lemon juice
    - 1/4 teaspoon ground cinnamon (optional)
- **For the Pastry:**
    - 1 sheet of puff pastry (store-bought or homemade)
    - Flour for dusting

Instructions:

1. **Preheat Oven:**
    - Preheat your oven to 375°F (190°C).
2. **Prepare the Caramel:**
    - In a heavy-bottomed skillet or ovenproof pan, heat the sugar over medium heat until it melts and turns a deep amber color. Avoid stirring too much to prevent crystallization.
    - Once the sugar has caramelized, add the butter and stir until smooth. Remove from heat.
3. **Prepare the Apples:**
    - Peel, core, and slice the apples into wedges.
    - Toss the apple slices with lemon juice and cinnamon if using.
4. **Assemble the Tarte:**
    - Arrange the apple slices in the caramel, packing them tightly as they will shrink during cooking.
    - Cook the apples in the caramel over medium heat for about 10-15 minutes, until they start to soften.
5. **Add the Pastry:**
    - Roll out the puff pastry on a lightly floured surface to fit the skillet or pan.
    - Place the pastry over the apples, tucking the edges down around the apples.
6. **Bake:**
    - Transfer the skillet to the preheated oven and bake for 25-30 minutes, or until the pastry is golden brown and puffed.
7. **Cool and Serve:**
    - Let the tart cool in the skillet for about 10 minutes.
    - Carefully invert the tart onto a plate. If some apples stick, just rearrange them.
8. **Enjoy:**
    - Serve warm or at room temperature. It pairs wonderfully with vanilla ice cream or whipped cream.

This recipe gives you a beautifully caramelized apple tart with a crisp pastry top.

Madeleines

Ingredients:

- **For the Madeleines:**
    - 1/2 cup (115g) unsalted butter, plus extra for greasing
    - 1 cup (130g) all-purpose flour
    - 1/2 cup (100g) granulated sugar
    - 2 large eggs
    - 1/2 teaspoon baking powder
    - 1/4 teaspoon salt
    - 1 teaspoon vanilla extract
    - Zest of 1 lemon (optional)
- **For Dusting:**
    - Powdered sugar (optional)

Instructions:

1. **Preheat Oven:**
    - Preheat your oven to 375°F (190°C).
2. **Prepare the Pan:**
    - Grease a madeleine pan with butter and lightly dust it with flour, or use a non-stick spray.
3. **Melt the Butter:**
    - In a small saucepan, melt the butter over low heat. Let it cool slightly.
4. **Mix Dry Ingredients:**
    - In a medium bowl, whisk together the flour, baking powder, and salt.
5. **Beat the Eggs and Sugar:**
    - In a large bowl, beat the eggs and granulated sugar with an electric mixer on medium speed until pale and thickened, about 3-4 minutes.
6. **Combine Ingredients:**
    - Gently fold the dry ingredients into the egg mixture using a spatula or wooden spoon until just combined.
    - Fold in the melted butter, vanilla extract, and lemon zest (if using), being careful not to overmix.
7. **Fill the Pan:**
    - Spoon the batter into the madeleine pan, filling each mold about 3/4 full.
8. **Bake:**
    - Bake for 10-12 minutes, or until the madeleines are golden brown and a toothpick inserted into the center comes out clean.
9. **Cool:**
    - Allow the madeleines to cool in the pan for a few minutes, then transfer them to a wire rack to cool completely.
10. **Dust and Serve:**
    - Optionally, dust the madeleines with powdered sugar before serving.

Madeleines are best enjoyed fresh but can be stored in an airtight container for a few days. They're perfect with tea or coffee!

Financiers

Ingredients:

- **For the Financiers:**
    - 1/2 cup (115g) unsalted butter
    - 1 cup (100g) almond flour (finely ground almonds)
    - 1 cup (125g) powdered sugar
    - 1/4 cup (30g) all-purpose flour
    - 1/4 teaspoon salt
    - 4 large egg whites
    - 1/2 teaspoon vanilla extract (optional)
- **For Garnish (optional):**
    - Fresh berries, sliced almonds, or a dusting of powdered sugar

Instructions:

1. **Preheat Oven:**
    - Preheat your oven to 375°F (190°C).
2. **Prepare the Butter:**
    - Melt the butter in a small saucepan over medium heat. Continue cooking until the butter turns golden brown and has a nutty aroma. Remove from heat and let it cool slightly.
3. **Mix Dry Ingredients:**
    - In a medium bowl, whisk together the almond flour, powdered sugar, all-purpose flour, and salt.
4. **Beat Egg Whites:**
    - In a large bowl, beat the egg whites with an electric mixer until they become frothy but not stiff (you don't need to form peaks).
5. **Combine Ingredients:**
    - Fold the dry ingredients into the egg whites until just combined.
    - Gently fold in the melted butter and vanilla extract, being careful not to overmix.
6. **Fill the Molds:**
    - Spoon the batter into greased financier molds or mini muffin pans, filling each about 3/4 full.
7. **Bake:**
    - Bake for 15-20 minutes, or until the financiers are golden brown and a toothpick inserted into the center comes out clean.
8. **Cool:**
    - Allow the financiers to cool in the pan for a few minutes, then transfer them to a wire rack to cool completely.
9. **Garnish and Serve:**
    - Optionally, garnish with fresh berries, sliced almonds, or a dusting of powdered sugar before serving.

Financiers are delightful on their own or paired with a cup of tea or coffee. Enjoy their light, nutty flavor and tender crumb!

Opéra Cake

Ingredients:

For the Joconde (Sponge Cake):

- 1/2 cup (50g) almond flour
- 1/2 cup (60g) all-purpose flour
- 1 cup (100g) powdered sugar
- 4 large eggs
- 4 large egg whites
- 1/4 cup (50g) granulated sugar
- 2 tablespoons (30g) unsalted butter, melted
- 1/2 teaspoon vanilla extract

For the Coffee Syrup:

- 1/2 cup (120ml) strong brewed coffee (cooled)
- 1/4 cup (50g) granulated sugar

For the Coffee Buttercream:

- 1/2 cup (115g) unsalted butter, room temperature
- 1/2 cup (60g) powdered sugar
- 2 tablespoons (30g) coffee extract or strong brewed coffee (cooled)

For the Chocolate Ganache:

- 1/2 cup (120ml) heavy cream
- 4 ounces (115g) semisweet or bittersweet chocolate, chopped

For the Chocolate Glaze:

- 1/2 cup (120ml) heavy cream
- 4 ounces (115g) semisweet or bittersweet chocolate, chopped

Instructions:

1. **Prepare the Joconde (Sponge Cake):**
    - Preheat your oven to 375°F (190°C). Line a baking sheet with parchment paper.
    - In a large bowl, whisk together almond flour, all-purpose flour, and powdered sugar.
    - In another bowl, beat the eggs until foamy, then fold into the dry ingredients.
    - In a separate bowl, whisk egg whites until soft peaks form. Gradually add granulated sugar and whisk until stiff peaks form.

- Gently fold the egg whites into the egg and flour mixture. Fold in melted butter and vanilla extract.
- Spread the batter evenly on the prepared baking sheet.
- Bake for 8-10 minutes, or until golden brown. Let it cool, then cut into three even rectangles.

2. **Prepare the Coffee Syrup:**
   - Combine coffee and granulated sugar in a small saucepan. Heat until the sugar dissolves. Allow to cool.
3. **Prepare the Coffee Buttercream:**
   - Beat butter until creamy. Gradually add powdered sugar and beat until light and fluffy.
   - Mix in coffee extract or brewed coffee until fully combined.
4. **Prepare the Chocolate Ganache:**
   - Heat the heavy cream in a small saucepan until it just begins to simmer. Pour over chopped chocolate in a bowl. Let it sit for a few minutes, then stir until smooth. Allow to cool slightly.
5. **Prepare the Chocolate Glaze:**
   - Heat the heavy cream in a small saucepan until it just begins to simmer. Pour over chopped chocolate in a bowl. Let it sit for a few minutes, then stir until smooth. Let it cool until slightly thickened.
6. **Assemble the Cake:**
   - Place one layer of Joconde on a serving plate. Brush generously with coffee syrup.
   - Spread a layer of coffee buttercream over the cake.
   - Add a layer of chocolate ganache and smooth it out.
   - Place the second layer of Joconde on top and repeat the layering process (coffee syrup, coffee buttercream, chocolate ganache).
   - Place the final layer of Joconde on top and chill the assembled cake in the refrigerator for at least 1 hour to set.
7. **Glaze the Cake:**
   - Pour the chocolate glaze over the chilled cake, spreading it evenly with a spatula.
   - Chill again until the glaze is set.
8. **Serve:**
   - Decorate with additional chocolate decorations if desired. Slice and serve.

Opéra Cake is rich and elegant, making it a perfect choice for special occasions or indulgent treats. Enjoy your baking!

Clafoutis

Ingredients:

- **For the Clafoutis:**
    - 2 cups (250g) pitted cherries (fresh or frozen)
    - 3 large eggs
    - 1 cup (240ml) whole milk
    - 1/2 cup (100g) granulated sugar
    - 1/4 cup (30g) all-purpose flour
    - 1/4 teaspoon salt
    - 1 teaspoon vanilla extract
    - 2 tablespoons (30g) unsalted butter, melted
    - Powdered sugar for dusting (optional)

Instructions:

1. **Preheat Oven:**
    - Preheat your oven to 350°F (175°C).
2. **Prepare the Fruit:**
    - If using fresh cherries, wash, pit, and halve them. If using frozen cherries, thaw and drain them well.
3. **Prepare the Pan:**
    - Butter a 9-inch (23cm) round baking dish or pie dish.
4. **Make the Batter:**
    - In a medium bowl, whisk together the eggs and granulated sugar until smooth.
    - Add the milk, flour, salt, and vanilla extract, and whisk until the batter is well combined and smooth.
    - Stir in the melted butter.
5. **Assemble the Clafoutis:**
    - Spread the cherries evenly in the bottom of the prepared baking dish.
    - Pour the batter over the cherries.
6. **Bake:**
    - Bake for 35-45 minutes, or until the clafoutis is puffed, golden brown, and a knife inserted into the center comes out clean.
7. **Cool and Serve:**
    - Allow the clafoutis to cool slightly before dusting with powdered sugar, if desired.
    - Serve warm or at room temperature.

Clafoutis is wonderfully adaptable—try it with other fruits like blueberries, raspberries, or sliced apples if you prefer. Enjoy this simple yet elegant French dessert!

Gâteau Basque

Ingredients:

For the Pastry Cream Filling:

- 1 1/2 cups (360ml) whole milk
- 1/2 cup (100g) granulated sugar
- 3 large egg yolks
- 2 tablespoons (20g) cornstarch
- 1 tablespoon (15g) unsalted butter
- 1 teaspoon vanilla extract

For the Dough:

- 2 1/2 cups (315g) all-purpose flour
- 1 cup (200g) granulated sugar
- 1/2 teaspoon baking powder
- 1/4 teaspoon salt
- 1 cup (225g) unsalted butter, cold and cut into small pieces
- 1 large egg
- 1 teaspoon vanilla extract
- 1 large egg yolk (for egg wash)

For the Filling (optional):

- 1/2 cup (160g) cherry or apricot jam (if not using pastry cream)

Instructions:

1. **Prepare the Pastry Cream:**
    - In a medium saucepan, heat the milk over medium heat until it's just about to boil. Remove from heat.
    - In a bowl, whisk together the egg yolks and granulated sugar until pale and thick.
    - Add the cornstarch and whisk until smooth.
    - Gradually pour the hot milk into the egg mixture, whisking constantly to temper the eggs.
    - Return the mixture to the saucepan and cook over medium heat, whisking constantly until it thickens and comes to a boil. Continue cooking for 1-2 minutes.
    - Remove from heat and stir in the butter and vanilla extract. Let it cool to room temperature, then refrigerate until chilled.
2. **Prepare the Dough:**
    - In a large bowl, whisk together the flour, sugar, baking powder, and salt.
    - Add the cold butter pieces and use a pastry cutter or your fingers to work the butter into the flour mixture until it resembles coarse crumbs.

- Stir in the egg and vanilla extract until the dough comes together. It will be somewhat crumbly.
- Divide the dough into two pieces, one slightly larger than the other. Flatten each into discs, wrap in plastic wrap, and refrigerate for at least 1 hour.

3. **Assemble the Gâteau Basque:**
    - Preheat your oven to 350°F (175°C).
    - On a floured surface, roll out the larger piece of dough into a circle about 1/8 inch (3mm) thick. Transfer it to a greased 9-inch (23cm) round cake pan or tart pan.
    - Spread the cooled pastry cream (or jam, if using) evenly over the dough in the pan.
    - Roll out the smaller piece of dough and place it over the filling. Trim any excess dough and press the edges to seal.
    - Brush the top with beaten egg yolk and score the top lightly with a knife in a decorative pattern.
4. **Bake:**
    - Bake for 35-40 minutes, or until the top is golden brown and the filling is set. Let it cool in the pan for 10 minutes, then transfer to a wire rack to cool completely.
5. **Serve:**
    - Gâteau Basque is best enjoyed at room temperature or slightly warmed. It can be served as is or with a dusting of powdered sugar.

This delightful pastry combines a buttery crust with a creamy filling, making it a charming and delicious treat!

Paris-Brest

Ingredients:

For the Choux Pastry:

- 1 cup (240ml) water
- 1/2 cup (115g) unsalted butter
- 1 tablespoon granulated sugar
- 1/4 teaspoon salt
- 1 cup (130g) all-purpose flour
- 4 large eggs

For the Praline Cream:

- 1 cup (240ml) heavy cream
- 1 cup (250g) praline paste (store-bought or homemade)
- 1/4 cup (50g) granulated sugar (optional, to taste)
- 1 teaspoon vanilla extract

For the Assembly:

- Powdered sugar for dusting
- Sliced almonds for topping

For the Homemade Praline Paste (optional):

- 1 cup (200g) granulated sugar
- 1 cup (120g) whole almonds

Instructions:

1. **Prepare the Praline Paste (if making homemade):**
   - Preheat your oven to 350°F (175°C).
   - Spread almonds on a baking sheet and toast in the oven for about 10 minutes, or until golden and fragrant.
   - In a saucepan, heat the granulated sugar over medium heat until it melts and turns a golden caramel color.
   - Stir in the toasted almonds and pour the mixture onto a parchment-lined baking sheet to cool completely.
   - Once cooled, break the caramel into pieces and blend in a food processor until smooth. This can be stored for up to 2 weeks.
2. **Make the Choux Pastry:**
   - Preheat your oven to 400°F (200°C).
   - In a medium saucepan, bring the water, butter, sugar, and salt to a boil.

- Remove from heat and add the flour all at once, stirring vigorously with a wooden spoon until the dough comes together and pulls away from the sides of the pan.
- Return to low heat and cook, stirring constantly, for 1-2 minutes to dry out the dough slightly.
- Transfer the dough to a bowl and let it cool slightly.
- Beat in the eggs one at a time, making sure each is fully incorporated before adding the next. The dough should be smooth and glossy.
- Transfer the dough to a piping bag fitted with a large round tip.

3. **Pipe and Bake:**
    - On a parchment-lined baking sheet, pipe a large ring of dough about 8 inches (20 cm) in diameter, making sure the ring is even.
    - Pipe a second ring on top of the first one to give it a higher profile.
    - Smooth the surface with a spatula or wet finger, and sprinkle with sliced almonds.
    - Bake for 30-35 minutes, or until golden brown and puffed. Let it cool completely on a wire rack.

4. **Prepare the Praline Cream:**
    - Whip the heavy cream until soft peaks form.
    - Fold in the praline paste and vanilla extract until fully combined. Taste and adjust sweetness with granulated sugar if needed.

5. **Assemble the Paris-Brest:**
    - Once the choux pastry is completely cool, slice it horizontally in half.
    - Fill the bottom half with the praline cream using a piping bag or a spoon.
    - Place the top half back on top of the cream.
    - Dust with powdered sugar before serving.

Paris-Brest is best enjoyed fresh, with its crisp pastry and creamy filling providing a delightful contrast.

Charlotte aux Fraises

Ingredients:

For the Strawberry Filling:

- 1 pound (450g) fresh strawberries, hulled and sliced
- 1/2 cup (100g) granulated sugar
- 1 teaspoon lemon juice
- 1 teaspoon vanilla extract
- 2 teaspoons gelatin powder or 4 gelatin sheets
- 1 cup (240ml) heavy cream

For the Ladyfingers:

- 24-30 ladyfingers (savoiardi), depending on the size of your mold

For the Assembly:

- Fresh strawberries for garnish
- Mint leaves for garnish (optional)

Instructions:

1. **Prepare the Strawberry Filling:**
   - In a medium saucepan, combine the sliced strawberries, granulated sugar, lemon juice, and vanilla extract. Cook over medium heat, stirring occasionally, until the strawberries release their juices and the mixture thickens slightly (about 10 minutes).
   - If using gelatin sheets, soak them in cold water for about 5 minutes, then squeeze out excess water. If using powdered gelatin, dissolve it in a small amount of hot water according to package instructions.
   - Remove the strawberry mixture from heat and stir in the gelatin until fully dissolved. Let the mixture cool to room temperature.
   - Whip the heavy cream to soft peaks and gently fold it into the cooled strawberry mixture until well combined.
2. **Prepare the Ladyfingers:**
   - Lightly grease a Charlotte mold or a 9-inch (23cm) round springform pan.
   - Arrange the ladyfingers in a single layer on a plate or in a shallow dish. Quickly dip each ladyfinger into a mixture of water and a bit of sugar or fruit juice (optional) to soften slightly, but do not soak them.
3. **Assemble the Charlotte:**
   - Line the sides of the prepared mold with the dipped ladyfingers, standing them upright and slightly overlapping. If using a springform pan, place the ladyfingers around the edges.
   - Spoon the strawberry mousse into the center of the mold, spreading it evenly.

- Top with additional ladyfingers if needed to cover the top of the filling.
4. **Chill:**
    - Cover the Charlotte with plastic wrap and refrigerate for at least 4 hours, or overnight, to allow it to set properly.
5. **Serve:**
    - Before serving, garnish the top with fresh strawberries and mint leaves if desired.
    - Carefully remove the Charlotte from the mold and place it on a serving plate.

Note: If you don't have a Charlotte mold, you can use a ring mold or a springform pan. For a richer version, you can add a layer of strawberry jelly or jam between the ladyfingers and mousse.

This dessert is perfect for showcasing seasonal strawberries and is sure to impress with its beautiful presentation and refreshing flavor!

Gâteau au Yaourt

Ingredients:

- 1 cup (240g) plain yogurt (whole milk or Greek yogurt works well)
- 1 cup (200g) granulated sugar
- 1/2 cup (120ml) vegetable oil or melted butter
- 3 large eggs
- 1 1/2 cups (190g) all-purpose flour
- 1 1/2 teaspoons baking powder
- 1/2 teaspoon baking soda
- 1/4 teaspoon salt
- 1 teaspoon vanilla extract (optional)
- Zest of 1 lemon or orange (optional)

Instructions:

1. **Preheat Oven:**
   - Preheat your oven to 350°F (175°C). Grease and flour a 9-inch (23cm) round cake pan or line it with parchment paper.
2. **Prepare the Batter:**
   - In a large bowl, whisk together the yogurt, sugar, and eggs until smooth and well combined.
   - Add the oil or melted butter and vanilla extract (if using) and mix well.
   - In a separate bowl, whisk together the flour, baking powder, baking soda, and salt.
   - Gradually add the dry ingredients to the wet ingredients, mixing until just combined. Avoid overmixing.
   - If using, fold in the lemon or orange zest.
3. **Bake:**
   - Pour the batter into the prepared cake pan and smooth the top with a spatula.
   - Bake for 30-35 minutes, or until a toothpick inserted into the center comes out clean and the cake is golden brown.
4. **Cool:**
   - Allow the cake to cool in the pan for about 10 minutes, then transfer it to a wire rack to cool completely.
5. **Serve:**
   - Dust with powdered sugar or serve with fresh fruit or a dollop of yogurt if desired.

Variations:

- **Fruit Add-ins:** You can fold in berries, apples, or other fruit for added flavor.
- **Spices:** Add a teaspoon of cinnamon or nutmeg for a spiced version.
- **Toppings:** Glaze with a simple lemon glaze or sprinkle with powdered sugar before serving.

This yogurt cake is delightful on its own or with a variety of toppings. Its simplicity and moist texture make it a perfect everyday treat!

Mille-feuille

Ingredients:

For the Puff Pastry:

- 1 sheet of store-bought puff pastry (or homemade, if preferred)

For the Pastry Cream:

- 2 cups (480ml) whole milk
- 1/2 cup (100g) granulated sugar
- 1/4 cup (30g) cornstarch
- 4 large egg yolks
- 2 tablespoons (30g) unsalted butter
- 1 teaspoon vanilla extract

For the Glaze:

- 1 cup (120g) powdered sugar
- 2-3 tablespoons water or milk
- 1 teaspoon vanilla extract

For Decoration (optional):

- Fresh berries
- Mint leaves
- Extra powdered sugar for dusting

Instructions:

1. **Prepare the Puff Pastry:**
    - Preheat your oven to 400°F (200°C). Line a baking sheet with parchment paper.
    - Roll out the puff pastry on a lightly floured surface to smooth it and slightly increase its size.
    - Cut the pastry into three equal rectangles (about 8x4 inches each). Place them on the prepared baking sheet.
    - Place another sheet of parchment paper on top of the pastry and weight it down with another baking sheet or some baking weights. This helps to keep the pastry from puffing too much.
    - Bake for 15-20 minutes, or until golden brown and crisp. Let the pastry cool completely.
2. **Make the Pastry Cream:**

- In a medium saucepan, heat the milk over medium heat until it just begins to simmer.
    - In a separate bowl, whisk together the sugar, cornstarch, and egg yolks until smooth.
    - Gradually pour the hot milk into the egg mixture, whisking constantly to temper the eggs.
    - Return the mixture to the saucepan and cook over medium heat, whisking constantly until it thickens and comes to a boil. Continue cooking for 1-2 minutes.
    - Remove from heat and stir in the butter and vanilla extract. Transfer the cream to a bowl, cover with plastic wrap (pressing the wrap directly onto the surface of the cream to prevent a skin from forming), and let it cool completely.
3. **Prepare the Glaze:**
    - In a small bowl, mix the powdered sugar with water or milk to create a smooth, spreadable glaze. Add vanilla extract and adjust the consistency if needed.
4. **Assemble the Mille-feuille:**
    - Once the puff pastry and pastry cream are completely cooled, spread a layer of pastry cream over one of the puff pastry rectangles.
    - Place another rectangle of pastry on top of the cream and spread with more cream.
    - Top with the final rectangle of pastry.
5. **Glaze and Decorate:**
    - Spread the glaze over the top layer of puff pastry.
    - Optionally, use a fork to create a decorative pattern on the glaze or dust with powdered sugar.
6. **Serve:**
    - Chill the assembled Mille-feuille in the refrigerator for about an hour to allow the cream to set and the flavors to meld.
    - Slice and serve. Garnish with fresh berries and mint leaves if desired.

Mille-feuille is a sophisticated dessert that combines flaky pastry with smooth pastry cream, creating a deliciously balanced treat. Enjoy!

Gâteau Saint-Honoré

Ingredients:

For the Pâte Brisée (Shortcrust Pastry):

- 1 1/4 cups (160g) all-purpose flour
- 1/4 cup (50g) granulated sugar
- 1/2 cup (115g) unsalted butter, cold and cut into small pieces
- 1 large egg yolk
- 1-2 tablespoons cold water

For the Puff Pastry:

- 1 sheet of store-bought puff pastry (or homemade, if preferred)

For the Choux Pastry:

- 1/2 cup (120ml) water
- 1/4 cup (60g) unsalted butter
- 1/2 cup (65g) all-purpose flour
- 2 large eggs
- 1/4 teaspoon salt

For the Caramel Cream:

- 1 cup (200g) granulated sugar
- 1/2 cup (120ml) heavy cream
- 1 cup (240ml) whole milk
- 3 large egg yolks
- 2 tablespoons (20g) cornstarch
- 1 teaspoon vanilla extract

For the Assembly:

- Whipped cream (for piping)
- Caramel sauce (optional, for drizzling)

Instructions:

1. **Prepare the Pâte Brisée:**
    - In a food processor, combine flour and sugar. Add the cold butter and pulse until the mixture resembles coarse crumbs.
    - Add the egg yolk and pulse until the dough begins to come together. If needed, add cold water, a tablespoon at a time, until the dough holds together.

- Form the dough into a disk, wrap in plastic wrap, and refrigerate for at least 1 hour.
- Roll out the dough on a lightly floured surface and fit it into a 9-inch (23cm) tart pan. Trim the edges and refrigerate again for 30 minutes.
- Preheat your oven to 375°F (190°C). Line the tart shell with parchment paper and bake for 15 minutes. Remove the parchment and bake for an additional 10 minutes until golden brown. Let it cool completely.

2. **Prepare the Puff Pastry:**
   - Roll out the puff pastry on a lightly floured surface. Cut out a circle slightly larger than your tart pan.
   - Place the puff pastry on a parchment-lined baking sheet and use a fork to prick it all over to prevent puffing.
   - Bake at 375°F (190°C) for 15-20 minutes, or until golden brown. Let it cool.

3. **Prepare the Choux Pastry:**
   - In a medium saucepan, bring the water and butter to a boil. Add the flour and salt all at once, stirring vigorously until the mixture forms a ball and pulls away from the sides of the pan.
   - Remove from heat and let it cool slightly. Beat in the eggs one at a time, making sure each is fully incorporated before adding the next.
   - Transfer the choux pastry to a piping bag fitted with a plain round tip. Pipe small mounds (about 1 inch in diameter) onto a parchment-lined baking sheet.
   - Bake at 400°F (200°C) for 20-25 minutes, or until golden brown. Let cool.

4. **Prepare the Caramel Cream:**
   - In a medium saucepan, heat the sugar over medium heat until it melts and turns a deep amber color. Carefully stir in the heavy cream (it will bubble vigorously). Remove from heat and let it cool.
   - In another saucepan, heat the milk until it just begins to simmer. In a bowl, whisk together the egg yolks and cornstarch until smooth.
   - Gradually add the hot milk to the egg mixture, whisking constantly. Return the mixture to the saucepan and cook over medium heat, whisking constantly until it thickens and comes to a boil.
   - Remove from heat and stir in the caramel sauce and vanilla extract. Let the caramel cream cool to room temperature.

5. **Assemble the Gâteau Saint-Honoré:**
   - Spread the caramel cream evenly over the baked pâte brisée.
   - Cut the puff pastry into a circle and place it on top of the caramel cream.
   - Pipe whipped cream in decorative rosettes around the edge of the puff pastry. Top each rosette with a choux pastry puff.
   - Optionally, drizzle additional caramel sauce over the top.

6. **Serve:**
   - Chill the assembled Gâteau Saint-Honoré in the refrigerator for at least 1 hour before serving to let the flavors meld.

This impressive dessert combines multiple textures and flavors, making it a spectacular treat for special occasions or as a showstopper at any gathering. Enjoy!

Tarte au Citron

Ingredients:

For the Tart Shell:

- 1 1/4 cups (160g) all-purpose flour
- 1/4 cup (50g) granulated sugar
- 1/2 cup (115g) unsalted butter, cold and cut into small pieces
- 1 large egg yolk
- 1-2 tablespoons cold water (as needed)

For the Lemon Filling:

- 1 cup (240ml) freshly squeezed lemon juice (about 4-6 lemons)
- 1 tablespoon lemon zest (from about 2 lemons)
- 1 cup (200g) granulated sugar
- 4 large eggs
- 1/2 cup (120ml) heavy cream

For the Meringue (optional):

- 3 large egg whites
- 1/4 teaspoon cream of tartar
- 1/2 cup (100g) granulated sugar
- 1/4 teaspoon vanilla extract

Instructions:

1. **Prepare the Tart Shell:**
   - In a food processor, combine flour and sugar. Add the cold butter pieces and pulse until the mixture resembles coarse crumbs.
   - Add the egg yolk and pulse until the dough begins to come together. If needed, add cold water a tablespoon at a time until the dough holds together.
   - Form the dough into a disk, wrap in plastic wrap, and refrigerate for at least 30 minutes.
   - Preheat your oven to 375°F (190°C). Roll out the dough on a lightly floured surface to fit a 9-inch (23cm) tart pan. Press the dough into the pan, trimming the edges. Refrigerate for another 30 minutes.
   - Line the tart shell with parchment paper and fill with baking weights or dried beans. Bake for 15 minutes. Remove the parchment and weights, and bake for an additional 10 minutes until the crust is golden. Let it cool completely.
2. **Prepare the Lemon Filling:**
   - In a medium bowl, whisk together the lemon juice, lemon zest, and sugar until the sugar is dissolved.
   - Add the eggs one at a time, whisking after each addition.

- Stir in the heavy cream until smooth.
 - Pour the lemon filling into the pre-baked tart shell.
3. **Bake the Tart:**
 - Bake the tart at 350°F (175°C) for 25-30 minutes, or until the filling is set and slightly jiggly in the center. The edges should be firm and the top lightly golden.
 - Let the tart cool completely on a wire rack. It can be chilled in the refrigerator for a few hours or overnight for better flavor and texture.
4. **Prepare the Meringue (optional):**
 - In a clean, dry bowl, beat the egg whites and cream of tartar with an electric mixer until soft peaks form.
 - Gradually add the sugar while continuing to beat until stiff, glossy peaks form. Add the vanilla extract and beat until combined.
 - Spread or pipe the meringue over the cooled lemon filling.
5. **Brown the Meringue (optional):**
 - If using meringue, you can lightly toast it using a kitchen torch or place the tart under a broiler for a minute or two until the meringue is golden brown. Watch it carefully to avoid burning.
6. **Serve:**
 - Slice the tart and serve as is, or garnish with additional lemon zest or fresh berries if desired.

This lemon tart combines a crisp, buttery crust with a tangy and creamy lemon filling, creating a deliciously balanced dessert that's perfect for any occasion!

Baba au Rhum

Ingredients:

For the Baba Dough:

- 1/4 cup (60ml) whole milk
- 1/4 cup (50g) granulated sugar
- 2 1/4 teaspoons (7g) active dry yeast
- 1/2 cup (115g) unsalted butter, softened
- 2 large eggs
- 1 1/2 cups (190g) all-purpose flour
- 1/4 teaspoon salt

For the Rum Syrup:

- 1 cup (200g) granulated sugar
- 1 cup (240ml) water
- 1/4 cup (60ml) dark rum
- 1 teaspoon vanilla extract (optional)

For the Whipped Cream:

- 1 cup (240ml) heavy cream
- 2 tablespoons powdered sugar
- 1 teaspoon vanilla extract

For Garnish (optional):

- Fresh fruit (e.g., berries, citrus segments)
- Mint leaves

Instructions:

1. **Prepare the Baba Dough:**
   - In a small saucepan, warm the milk until it is lukewarm. Stir in the sugar and yeast. Let it sit for about 5 minutes until it becomes frothy.
   - In a large bowl or stand mixer, cream the softened butter until smooth. Add the eggs, one at a time, beating well after each addition.
   - Add the yeast mixture and mix until combined.
   - Gradually add the flour and salt, mixing until the dough is smooth and elastic. It will be somewhat sticky.
   - Cover the bowl with plastic wrap or a damp cloth and let it rise in a warm place for about 1 hour, or until doubled in size.
2. **Bake the Babas:**
   - Preheat your oven to 375°F (190°C). Grease and flour baba molds or a muffin tin.

- Punch down the dough and divide it evenly among the molds, filling them about two-thirds full.
- Let the dough rise again in the molds for about 30 minutes.
- Bake for 15-20 minutes, or until the babas are golden brown and a toothpick inserted into the center comes out clean. Let them cool slightly in the molds before transferring them to a wire rack.

3. **Prepare the Rum Syrup:**
   - In a medium saucepan, combine the sugar and water. Bring to a boil, stirring until the sugar is dissolved.
   - Remove from heat and stir in the rum and vanilla extract, if using. Allow the syrup to cool slightly.

4. **Soak the Babas:**
   - Once the babas have cooled slightly but are still warm, immerse them in the warm rum syrup for about 30 seconds to 1 minute, or until they are well-soaked. You can use a spoon to help pour syrup over the top if needed.
   - Let the soaked babas drain on a wire rack.

5. **Prepare the Whipped Cream:**
   - In a mixing bowl, whip the heavy cream with the powdered sugar and vanilla extract until stiff peaks form.

6. **Assemble and Serve:**
   - Place the babas on serving plates or in individual dishes.
   - Top each baba with a dollop of whipped cream.
   - Garnish with fresh fruit and mint leaves if desired.

Tip: Baba au Rhum can be served warm or at room temperature. For an extra touch of indulgence, you can also serve it with a side of crème anglaise or a scoop of vanilla ice cream.

This dessert offers a wonderful combination of flavors and textures, with the rich rum-soaked cake and the light, fluffy whipped cream complementing each other perfectly. Enjoy!

Pithiviers

Ingredients:

For the Puff Pastry:

- 1 sheet of store-bought puff pastry (or homemade, if preferred)

For the Almond Filling:

- 1/2 cup (100g) granulated sugar
- 1/2 cup (100g) unsalted butter, softened
- 1 cup (100g) almond flour (ground almonds)
- 2 large eggs
- 1 teaspoon vanilla extract
- 2 tablespoons (30ml) dark rum or cognac (optional)

For the Assembly:

- 1 egg, beaten (for egg wash)
- Powdered sugar (for dusting, optional)

Instructions:

1. **Prepare the Almond Filling:**
    - In a medium bowl, cream together the granulated sugar and softened butter until light and fluffy.
    - Stir in the almond flour until well combined.
    - Beat in the eggs, one at a time, mixing well after each addition.
    - Add the vanilla extract and dark rum or cognac (if using), and mix until smooth.
2. **Prepare the Puff Pastry:**
    - Preheat your oven to 375°F (190°C).
    - Roll out the puff pastry on a lightly floured surface. If using store-bought puff pastry, you may need to roll it slightly to even it out.
    - Cut the pastry into two circles, each about 8-9 inches (20-23 cm) in diameter.
3. **Assemble the Pithiviers:**
    - Place one pastry circle on a baking sheet lined with parchment paper.
    - Spread the almond filling evenly over the center of the pastry, leaving a border of about 1 inch (2.5 cm) around the edge.
    - Brush the border with a little of the beaten egg.
    - Place the second pastry circle on top of the filling. Press down around the edges to seal and crimp the edges with a fork or your fingers.
    - Use a sharp knife to lightly score the top of the pastry in a decorative pattern, taking care not to cut through the pastry.
    - Brush the top with the remaining beaten egg to give it a shiny, golden finish.
4. **Bake the Pithiviers:**
    - Bake for 25-30 minutes, or until the pastry is golden brown and puffed up.

- Let it cool slightly before serving. If desired, dust with powdered sugar before serving.

Note: Pithiviers is often enjoyed warm or at room temperature. It's a delightful treat for special occasions or as a delicious dessert to accompany a cup of coffee or tea.

This pastry combines the rich, nutty flavor of almonds with the buttery crispiness of puff pastry, making it a luxurious and satisfying dessert. Enjoy!

Galette des Rois

Ingredients:

For the Almond Cream (Frangipane):

- 1/2 cup (100g) granulated sugar
- 1/2 cup (100g) unsalted butter, softened
- 1 cup (100g) almond flour (ground almonds)
- 2 large eggs
- 1 tablespoon all-purpose flour
- 1 teaspoon vanilla extract
- 1 tablespoon dark rum or cognac (optional)

For the Galette:

- 2 sheets of store-bought puff pastry (thawed if frozen)
- 1 egg, beaten (for egg wash)
- 1 fève (optional, but traditional)
- Powdered sugar (for dusting, optional)

Instructions:

1. **Prepare the Almond Cream (Frangipane):**
   - In a medium bowl, cream together the granulated sugar and softened butter until light and fluffy.
   - Stir in the almond flour until well combined.
   - Beat in the eggs, one at a time, mixing well after each addition.
   - Add the flour, vanilla extract, and dark rum or cognac (if using). Mix until smooth. Set aside.
2. **Prepare the Galette:**
   - Preheat your oven to 375°F (190°C). Line a baking sheet with parchment paper.
   - Roll out the puff pastry sheets on a lightly floured surface. If needed, trim them to fit your baking sheet.
   - Place one pastry sheet on the prepared baking sheet.
   - Spread the almond cream evenly over the pastry, leaving a border of about 1 inch (2.5 cm) around the edges.
   - If using, place the fève somewhere in the almond cream (be sure to notify your guests that there's a fève inside!).
   - Brush the border with some of the beaten egg.
   - Place the second pastry sheet on top and press down around the edges to seal. Crimp the edges with a fork or your fingers.
   - Use a sharp knife to lightly score the top of the galette in a decorative pattern, such as a spiral or diagonal lines. Be careful not to cut through the pastry.
   - Brush the top with the remaining beaten egg for a shiny, golden finish.
3. **Bake the Galette:**
   - Bake for 25-30 minutes, or until the pastry is golden brown and puffed up.

- Let it cool slightly before serving. If desired, dust with powdered sugar before serving.

Note: The Galette des Rois is traditionally enjoyed at room temperature or slightly warm. It's a delightful and festive treat that brings a touch of French tradition to your celebrations.

Enjoy your Galette des Rois with a cup of tea or coffee and celebrate Epiphany in style!

Choux à la Crème

Ingredients:

For the Choux Pastry:

- 1/2 cup (120ml) water
- 1/4 cup (60g) unsalted butter
- 1/4 teaspoon salt
- 1/2 cup (65g) all-purpose flour
- 2 large eggs

For the Cream Filling:

- 1 cup (240ml) heavy cream
- 1/4 cup (50g) granulated sugar
- 1 teaspoon vanilla extract

For the Optional Glaze (for a touch of elegance):

- 1/2 cup (60g) powdered sugar
- 1-2 tablespoons milk
- 1/2 teaspoon vanilla extract

Instructions:

1. **Prepare the Choux Pastry:**
    - Preheat your oven to 425°F (220°C). Line a baking sheet with parchment paper.
    - In a medium saucepan, combine the water, butter, and salt. Bring to a boil over medium heat, stirring occasionally.
    - Once the butter has melted and the mixture is boiling, remove the saucepan from the heat and immediately add the flour. Stir vigorously with a wooden spoon or spatula until the mixture forms a smooth dough and pulls away from the sides of the pan.
    - Return the saucepan to the heat and cook the dough for an additional 1-2 minutes, stirring constantly, to dry it out slightly.
    - Transfer the dough to a mixing bowl and let it cool for a few minutes.
    - Beat in the eggs, one at a time, until the dough is smooth and glossy. The dough should be thick but drop from a spoon when stirred.
    - Using a piping bag fitted with a plain round tip or a spoon, pipe or drop small mounds of dough (about 1 inch or 2.5 cm in diameter) onto the prepared baking sheet, spacing them about 2 inches (5 cm) apart.
    - Bake for 20-25 minutes, or until the puffs are golden brown and puffed up. Do not open the oven door while baking, as this can cause the puffs to collapse.
    - Once baked, turn off the oven and let the puffs cool inside with the door slightly ajar to prevent them from deflating. Cool completely on a wire rack.
2. **Prepare the Cream Filling:**

- In a medium bowl, beat the heavy cream, granulated sugar, and vanilla extract until stiff peaks form.
- Transfer the whipped cream to a piping bag fitted with a plain round tip.

3. **Assemble the Choux à la Crème:**
   - Once the choux puffs are completely cool, use a sharp knife or a small serrated knife to cut a small slit in the side of each puff or cut the tops off.
   - Pipe or spoon the whipped cream into each puff. If you cut off the tops, place them back on top after filling.

4. **Optional Glaze:**
   - In a small bowl, mix the powdered sugar with enough milk to create a smooth, drizzling consistency. Stir in the vanilla extract.
   - Drizzle the glaze over the filled cream puffs or dip the tops into the glaze.

5. **Serve:**
   - Choux à la Crème are best enjoyed fresh but can be stored in an airtight container for a day or two. They are perfect as a light dessert or a special treat.

This classic French pastry is both delicious and visually appealing, making it a wonderful addition to any dessert table. Enjoy your Choux à la Crème!

Gâteau de Mamie

Ingredients:

For the Cake:

- 1 1/2 cups (190g) all-purpose flour
- 1 cup (200g) granulated sugar
- 1/2 cup (115g) unsalted butter, softened
- 3 large eggs
- 1/2 cup (120ml) whole milk
- 1 teaspoon vanilla extract
- 1 1/2 teaspoons baking powder
- 1/4 teaspoon salt

For Optional Flavor Variations:

- **Lemon:** Zest of 1 lemon and 2 tablespoons lemon juice
- **Almond:** 1/2 teaspoon almond extract and 1/4 cup (25g) slivered almonds for topping
- **Chocolate:** 1/2 cup (85g) chocolate chips or chunks

For the Glaze (optional):

- 1 cup (120g) powdered sugar
- 2-3 tablespoons milk
- 1/2 teaspoon vanilla extract

Instructions:

1. **Preheat the Oven:**
    - Preheat your oven to 350°F (175°C). Grease and flour a 9-inch (23cm) round cake pan or line it with parchment paper.
2. **Prepare the Cake Batter:**
    - In a medium bowl, whisk together the flour, baking powder, and salt.
    - In a large bowl, cream the softened butter and granulated sugar until light and fluffy.
    - Add the eggs one at a time, beating well after each addition. Stir in the vanilla extract.
    - Gradually add the flour mixture to the butter mixture, alternating with the milk, beginning and ending with the flour mixture. Mix until just combined.
    - If adding any flavor variations (lemon zest and juice, almond extract, or chocolate chips), fold them into the batter now.
3. **Bake the Cake:**
    - Pour the batter into the prepared cake pan and smooth the top with a spatula.
    - Bake for 30-35 minutes, or until a toothpick inserted into the center of the cake comes out clean and the cake is golden brown on top.

- Let the cake cool in the pan for 10 minutes, then transfer it to a wire rack to cool completely.
4. **Prepare the Glaze (optional):**
    - In a small bowl, whisk together the powdered sugar, milk, and vanilla extract until smooth and drizzle-able.
    - Drizzle the glaze over the cooled cake, letting it set before serving.
5. **Serve:**
    - Slice and serve the cake as a delicious treat with coffee or tea. It's perfect for breakfast, a snack, or a simple dessert.

Notes:

- This cake is quite versatile and can be customized with different flavorings or add-ins based on your preference or what you have on hand.
- Gâteau de Mamie is best enjoyed fresh but can be stored in an airtight container at room temperature for a few days.

This classic cake embodies the comforting simplicity and love often associated with grandmother's recipes. Enjoy baking and savoring this delightful treat!

Tarte aux Pommes

Ingredients:

For the Pastry:

- 1 1/4 cups (160g) all-purpose flour
- 1/4 cup (50g) granulated sugar
- 1/2 cup (115g) unsalted butter, cold and cut into small pieces
- 1 large egg yolk
- 1-2 tablespoons cold water (as needed)

For the Apple Filling:

- 4-5 medium apples (such as Granny Smith, Honeycrisp, or any tart-sweet variety)
- 1/4 cup (50g) granulated sugar
- 1/2 teaspoon ground cinnamon
- 2 tablespoons unsalted butter
- 1 tablespoon lemon juice (optional)
- 1 tablespoon all-purpose flour (optional, for thickening)

For the Glaze (optional):

- 1/4 cup (60ml) apricot or apple jelly
- 1 tablespoon water

Instructions:

1. **Prepare the Pastry:**
   - In a food processor, combine the flour and sugar. Add the cold butter and pulse until the mixture resembles coarse crumbs.
   - Add the egg yolk and pulse until the dough begins to come together. If needed, add cold water a tablespoon at a time until the dough holds together.
   - Form the dough into a disk, wrap it in plastic wrap, and refrigerate for at least 30 minutes.
   - Preheat your oven to 375°F (190°C). Roll out the dough on a lightly floured surface to fit a 9-inch (23cm) tart pan. Press the dough into the pan and trim the edges. Prick the bottom with a fork to prevent bubbling. Chill for an additional 15 minutes.
2. **Blind Bake the Pastry:**
   - Line the pastry with parchment paper and fill with baking weights or dried beans.
   - Bake for 15 minutes. Remove the parchment and weights, and bake for another 10 minutes or until the crust is golden brown. Let it cool.
3. **Prepare the Apple Filling:**
   - Peel, core, and slice the apples thinly (about 1/8-inch thick). If using lemon juice, toss the apple slices with lemon juice to prevent browning.

- In a large skillet, melt the butter over medium heat. Add the apple slices, sugar, and cinnamon. Cook for 10-15 minutes, stirring occasionally, until the apples are tender and slightly caramelized. If the mixture is too liquid, you can stir in a tablespoon of flour to thicken it.

4. **Assemble the Tart:**
    - Spread the cooked apples evenly over the baked tart shell.
    - Arrange the apples in a decorative pattern, if desired, to make the tart visually appealing.
5. **Bake the Tart:**
    - Bake the tart at 375°F (190°C) for about 20-25 minutes, or until the apples are fully cooked and the tart is golden.
6. **Prepare the Glaze (optional):**
    - In a small saucepan, heat the apricot or apple jelly with water until melted and smooth. Brush the glaze over the apples to give them a shiny finish.
7. **Serve:**
    - Let the tart cool before slicing. It can be enjoyed warm or at room temperature. It pairs beautifully with a dollop of crème fraîche or a scoop of vanilla ice cream.

Tips:

- **Apple Selection:** Use apples that hold their shape well when baked, such as Granny Smith, Honeycrisp, or Fuji.
- **Texture:** For a different texture, you can slice the apples thickly or arrange them in a spiral pattern for a classic look.

This Tarte aux Pommes is a delightful, comforting dessert that showcases the flavors of fresh apples and a buttery crust. Enjoy baking and savoring this classic French treat!

Gâteau au Chocolat

Ingredients:

For the Cake:

- 1/2 cup (115g) unsalted butter
- 4 oz (115g) bittersweet or semi-sweet chocolate, chopped
- 1 cup (200g) granulated sugar
- 1/4 cup (50g) packed brown sugar
- 3 large eggs
- 1 teaspoon vanilla extract
- 1/2 cup (65g) all-purpose flour
- 1/4 cup (30g) unsweetened cocoa powder
- 1/4 teaspoon salt

For the Optional Ganache (for frosting):

- 6 oz (170g) bittersweet or semi-sweet chocolate, chopped
- 1/2 cup (120ml) heavy cream
- 2 tablespoons unsalted butter

For Garnish (optional):

- Fresh berries (e.g., raspberries, strawberries)
- Powdered sugar
- Whipped cream

Instructions:

1. **Prepare the Cake:**
    - Preheat your oven to 350°F (175°C). Grease and flour an 8-inch (20cm) round cake pan, or line it with parchment paper.
    - In a medium saucepan, melt the butter and chopped chocolate over low heat, stirring constantly until smooth. Remove from heat and let it cool slightly.
    - In a large bowl, whisk together the granulated sugar and brown sugar. Add the eggs one at a time, beating well after each addition. Stir in the vanilla extract.
    - Gradually add the melted chocolate mixture to the sugar and egg mixture, mixing until smooth.
    - Sift together the flour, cocoa powder, and salt. Fold the dry ingredients into the wet ingredients until just combined.
    - Pour the batter into the prepared cake pan and smooth the top with a spatula.
2. **Bake the Cake:**
    - Bake for 25-30 minutes, or until a toothpick inserted into the center comes out with a few moist crumbs. The cake should be set around the edges but slightly soft in the center.

- Let the cake cool in the pan for 10 minutes before transferring it to a wire rack to cool completely.
3. **Prepare the Ganache (optional):**
   - In a small saucepan, heat the heavy cream over medium heat until it begins to simmer. Remove from heat and add the chopped chocolate. Let it sit for a few minutes, then stir until smooth.
   - Stir in the butter until fully incorporated and the ganache is glossy. Let it cool slightly until it thickens to a spreadable consistency.
4. **Frost the Cake (optional):**
   - Once the cake is completely cool, spread or pipe the ganache over the top and sides of the cake.
   - Garnish with fresh berries, a dusting of powdered sugar, or a dollop of whipped cream, if desired.
5. **Serve:**
   - Slice and serve the cake at room temperature. It pairs wonderfully with a cup of coffee or a glass of dessert wine.

Tips:

- **Texture:** For a denser, more fudgy cake, you can reduce the flour slightly or add an extra egg.
- **Flavor:** You can add a pinch of espresso powder to the batter to enhance the chocolate flavor.
- **Storage:** The cake can be stored in an airtight container at room temperature for up to 3 days or refrigerated for up to a week.

This Gâteau au Chocolat is rich, indulgent, and sure to satisfy any chocolate lover. Enjoy making and savoring this classic French dessert!

Tarte Bourdaloue

Ingredients:

For the Pastry:

- 1 1/4 cups (160g) all-purpose flour
- 1/4 cup (50g) granulated sugar
- 1/2 cup (115g) unsalted butter, cold and cut into small pieces
- 1 large egg yolk
- 1-2 tablespoons cold water (as needed)

For the Almond Cream (Frangipane):

- 1/2 cup (100g) granulated sugar
- 1/2 cup (100g) unsalted butter, softened
- 1 cup (100g) almond flour (ground almonds)
- 2 large eggs
- 1 teaspoon vanilla extract
- 1 tablespoon all-purpose flour

For the Poached Pears:

- 2-3 ripe pears (e.g., Bosc or Anjou)
- 2 cups (480ml) water
- 1 cup (200g) granulated sugar
- 1/2 cup (120ml) white wine (optional)
- 1 cinnamon stick
- 1-2 strips of lemon zest

For the Garnish (optional):

- Sliced almonds
- Powdered sugar (for dusting)

Instructions:

1. **Prepare the Pastry:**
   - In a food processor, combine the flour and sugar. Add the cold butter and pulse until the mixture resembles coarse crumbs.
   - Add the egg yolk and pulse until the dough begins to come together. If needed, add cold water a tablespoon at a time until the dough holds together.
   - Form the dough into a disk, wrap it in plastic wrap, and refrigerate for at least 30 minutes.

- Preheat your oven to 375°F (190°C). Roll out the dough on a lightly floured surface to fit a 9-inch (23cm) tart pan. Press the dough into the pan and trim the edges. Prick the bottom with a fork.
- Chill the pastry shell for an additional 15 minutes.

2. **Blind Bake the Pastry:**
   - Line the pastry with parchment paper and fill with baking weights or dried beans.
   - Bake for 15 minutes. Remove the parchment and weights, and bake for another 10 minutes or until the crust is golden brown. Let it cool.

3. **Prepare the Almond Cream:**
   - In a medium bowl, cream together the granulated sugar and softened butter until light and fluffy.
   - Stir in the almond flour until well combined.
   - Beat in the eggs, one at a time, mixing well after each addition.
   - Add the vanilla extract and flour, mixing until smooth.

4. **Prepare the Poached Pears:**
   - Peel, core, and slice the pears into thin slices.
   - In a saucepan, combine the water, granulated sugar, white wine (if using), cinnamon stick, and lemon zest. Bring to a boil, stirring to dissolve the sugar.
   - Add the pear slices and simmer for 10-15 minutes, or until the pears are tender but still hold their shape.
   - Remove the pears from the poaching liquid and let them cool.

5. **Assemble the Tart:**
   - Spread the almond cream evenly over the cooled pastry shell.
   - Arrange the poached pear slices on top of the almond cream in a decorative pattern.
   - Bake the tart at 375°F (190°C) for 30-35 minutes, or until the almond cream is set and golden brown.

6. **Garnish and Serve:**
   - If desired, sprinkle the tart with sliced almonds and a dusting of powdered sugar before serving.
   - Let the tart cool before slicing and serving. It can be enjoyed warm or at room temperature.

Tips:

- **Poaching Liquid:** The poaching liquid can be reduced and used as a syrup to drizzle over the tart or serve alongside it.
- **Pastry:** Make sure the pastry is well-chilled before baking to avoid shrinking.
- **Almond Cream:** If you prefer a more intense almond flavor, you can add a few drops of almond extract to the almond cream mixture.

Tarte Bourdaloue is a refined and delicious dessert that pairs beautifully with a cup of coffee or tea. Enjoy making and indulging in this classic French tart!

Tarte aux Framboises

Ingredients:

For the Pastry:

- 1 1/4 cups (160g) all-purpose flour
- 1/4 cup (50g) granulated sugar
- 1/2 cup (115g) unsalted butter, cold and cut into small pieces
- 1 large egg yolk
- 1-2 tablespoons cold water (as needed)

For the Almond Cream (Frangipane):

- 1/2 cup (100g) granulated sugar
- 1/2 cup (100g) unsalted butter, softened
- 1 cup (100g) almond flour (ground almonds)
- 2 large eggs
- 1 teaspoon vanilla extract
- 1 tablespoon all-purpose flour

For the Raspberry Topping:

- 1-2 cups (150-300g) fresh raspberries
- 1/4 cup (50g) granulated sugar (optional, for sprinkling over raspberries)
- Powdered sugar (for dusting, optional)

For the Glaze (optional):

- 1/4 cup (60ml) apricot or raspberry jelly
- 1 tablespoon water

Instructions:

1. **Prepare the Pastry:**
   - In a food processor, combine the flour and sugar. Add the cold butter and pulse until the mixture resembles coarse crumbs.
   - Add the egg yolk and pulse until the dough starts to come together. If needed, add cold water a tablespoon at a time until the dough holds together.
   - Form the dough into a disk, wrap it in plastic wrap, and refrigerate for at least 30 minutes.
   - Preheat your oven to 375°F (190°C). Roll out the dough on a lightly floured surface to fit a 9-inch (23cm) tart pan. Press the dough into the pan and trim the edges. Prick the bottom with a fork.
   - Chill the pastry shell for an additional 15 minutes.
2. **Blind Bake the Pastry:**

- Line the pastry with parchment paper and fill with baking weights or dried beans.
        - Bake for 15 minutes. Remove the parchment and weights, and bake for another 10 minutes or until the crust is golden brown. Let it cool.
3. **Prepare the Almond Cream:**
    - In a medium bowl, cream together the granulated sugar and softened butter until light and fluffy.
    - Stir in the almond flour until well combined.
    - Beat in the eggs, one at a time, mixing well after each addition.
    - Add the vanilla extract and flour, mixing until smooth.
4. **Assemble the Tart:**
    - Spread the almond cream evenly over the cooled pastry shell.
    - Bake at 375°F (190°C) for 25-30 minutes, or until the almond cream is set and golden brown. Let it cool completely.
5. **Top with Raspberries:**
    - Once the tart is cool, arrange the fresh raspberries on top of the almond cream in a decorative pattern.
    - If desired, sprinkle the raspberries with a little granulated sugar to enhance their sweetness.
6. **Prepare the Glaze (optional):**
    - In a small saucepan, heat the apricot or raspberry jelly with water until melted and smooth. Brush the glaze over the raspberries to give them a shiny finish.
7. **Serve:**
    - Dust the tart with powdered sugar before serving, if desired.
    - Slice and serve the tart chilled or at room temperature. It pairs wonderfully with a cup of tea or a glass of dessert wine.

Tips:

- **Fresh Raspberries:** For the best results, use fresh raspberries, as frozen ones can release excess moisture and affect the tart's texture.
- **Almond Cream:** You can add a touch of almond extract to the almond cream for a more intense almond flavor.
- **Storage:** The tart can be stored in the refrigerator for a few days, but it's best enjoyed fresh.

This Tarte aux Framboises is a beautiful and delicious way to enjoy raspberries and a classic example of French pastry perfection. Enjoy making and savoring this elegant tart!

Gâteau Mont-Blanc

Ingredients:

For the Sponge Cake:

- 4 large eggs
- 1 cup (200g) granulated sugar
- 1 cup (120g) all-purpose flour
- 1/2 teaspoon baking powder
- 1/4 cup (60ml) milk
- 1/4 cup (60g) unsalted butter, melted
- 1 teaspoon vanilla extract

For the Chestnut Cream Filling:

- 1 cup (240ml) heavy cream
- 1 cup (250g) chestnut purée (sweetened, can be found in jars or cans)
- 1/4 cup (50g) granulated sugar
- 1 tablespoon rum or brandy (optional)
- 1 teaspoon vanilla extract

For the Whipped Cream Topping:

- 1 cup (240ml) heavy cream
- 2 tablespoons powdered sugar
- 1 teaspoon vanilla extract

For Garnish:

- Shredded or chopped candied chestnuts
- Cocoa powder or powdered sugar for dusting

Instructions:

1. **Prepare the Sponge Cake:**
   - Preheat your oven to 350°F (175°C). Grease and flour two 8-inch (20cm) round cake pans or line them with parchment paper.
   - In a large bowl, beat the eggs and granulated sugar together until light and fluffy.
   - Sift the flour and baking powder together and fold into the egg mixture, alternating with the milk.
   - Gently fold in the melted butter and vanilla extract until smooth.
   - Divide the batter evenly between the prepared pans and smooth the tops.
   - Bake for 20-25 minutes, or until a toothpick inserted into the center comes out clean. Let the cakes cool in the pans for 10 minutes before transferring them to a wire rack to cool completely.

2. **Prepare the Chestnut Cream Filling:**
   - In a medium bowl, whip the heavy cream until soft peaks form.
   - Fold the chestnut purée into the whipped cream until well combined. Add granulated sugar, rum or brandy (if using), and vanilla extract. Mix gently until smooth.
3. **Assemble the Cake:**
   - If the sponge cakes have domed tops, level them with a knife so they are flat.
   - Place one layer of sponge cake on a serving plate. Spread a generous layer of chestnut cream filling over the top.
   - Place the second sponge cake layer on top of the chestnut cream and press down gently.
4. **Prepare the Whipped Cream Topping:**
   - In a clean bowl, whip the heavy cream with powdered sugar and vanilla extract until stiff peaks form.
   - Spread or pipe the whipped cream over the top and sides of the cake.
5. **Garnish and Serve:**
   - Garnish the top of the cake with shredded or chopped candied chestnuts and a light dusting of cocoa powder or powdered sugar.
   - Chill the cake in the refrigerator for at least an hour before serving to let the flavors meld and the cake set.

Tips:

- **Chestnut Purée:** Make sure to use sweetened chestnut purée. If it's unsweetened, you might need to adjust the amount of sugar in the chestnut cream.
- **Whipped Cream:** For a stiffer whipped cream that holds its shape better, make sure the cream and mixing bowl are very cold.
- **Decoration:** You can also decorate with additional elements like chocolate shavings or fresh berries for extra flair.

Gâteau Mont-Blanc is a rich and elegant dessert that beautifully combines the flavors of chestnut and cream. It's perfect for special occasions or as a treat to impress your guests. Enjoy baking and savoring this luxurious French cake!

Crêpes Suzette

Ingredients:

For the Crêpes:

- 1 cup (125g) all-purpose flour
- 2 large eggs
- 1 cup (240ml) milk
- 2 tablespoons granulated sugar
- 1/4 teaspoon salt
- 2 tablespoons unsalted butter, melted
- 1 teaspoon vanilla extract (optional)

For the Orange Sauce:

- 1/2 cup (120ml) fresh orange juice
- 1/4 cup (60ml) freshly squeezed lemon juice
- 1/4 cup (50g) granulated sugar
- 2 tablespoons unsalted butter
- 1 tablespoon orange zest
- 1 tablespoon orange liqueur (e.g., Grand Marnier, Cointreau) or cognac
- 2 tablespoons water (if needed)

For Flambéing (optional):

- 2 tablespoons orange liqueur (e.g., Grand Marnier, Cointreau) or cognac

Instructions:

1. **Prepare the Crêpe Batter:**
   - In a large mixing bowl, whisk together the flour, eggs, milk, sugar, and salt until smooth. Stir in the melted butter and vanilla extract if using.
   - Let the batter rest for at least 30 minutes at room temperature. This helps the crêpes cook more evenly.
2. **Cook the Crêpes:**
   - Heat a non-stick skillet or crêpe pan over medium heat and lightly grease with butter or oil.
   - Pour a small amount of batter into the pan and quickly tilt and swirl to spread it evenly. Cook for about 1-2 minutes, or until the edges start to lift and the bottom is golden brown.
   - Flip the crêpe and cook for another 30 seconds to 1 minute. Transfer to a plate and repeat with the remaining batter.
   - Stack the cooked crêpes and keep warm.
3. **Prepare the Orange Sauce:**

- In a small saucepan, combine the orange juice, lemon juice, sugar, and orange zest. Bring to a simmer over medium heat.
- Cook until the mixture reduces by about half and becomes slightly syrupy (about 5-7 minutes).
- Stir in the butter until melted and incorporated. If the sauce is too thick, add a little water to reach the desired consistency.
- Remove from heat and stir in the orange liqueur.

4. **Assemble the Crêpes Suzette:**
   - Fold each crêpe into quarters or roll them up and arrange them on a serving plate.
   - Spoon the warm orange sauce over the crêpes.
5. **Flambé (optional):**
   - In a small saucepan, heat the orange liqueur or cognac until warm but not boiling.
   - Carefully ignite the liqueur with a long lighter and pour it over the crêpes, allowing the flames to subside. If you're not comfortable with flambéing, you can skip this step and simply serve the crêpes with the sauce.
6. **Serve:**
   - Serve the Crêpes Suzette immediately, garnished with extra orange zest if desired.

Tips:

- **Crêpe Pan:** A non-stick crêpe pan or skillet works best for making thin, evenly cooked crêpes.
- **Resting the Batter:** Resting the batter helps to achieve a smoother consistency and better texture in the crêpes.
- **Flambéing:** Ensure you use a long lighter and keep a safe distance when flambéing. Alternatively, you can skip flambéing and simply serve the crêpes with the sauce.

Crêpes Suzette is a luxurious and impressive dessert that combines the delicate texture of crêpes with a tangy orange sauce. Enjoy this classic French treat that's sure to impress your guests!

Tarte au Chocolat

Ingredients:

For the Pastry:

- 1 1/4 cups (160g) all-purpose flour
- 1/4 cup (50g) granulated sugar
- 1/2 cup (115g) unsalted butter, cold and cut into small pieces
- 1 large egg yolk
- 1-2 tablespoons cold water (as needed)

For the Chocolate Ganache Filling:

- 1 cup (240ml) heavy cream
- 8 oz (225g) bittersweet or semi-sweet chocolate, chopped
- 2 tablespoons unsalted butter
- 1 teaspoon vanilla extract (optional)

For Garnish (optional):

- Fresh berries (e.g., raspberries, strawberries)
- Whipped cream
- Chocolate shavings or curls
- Powdered sugar (for dusting)

Instructions:

1. **Prepare the Pastry:**
    - In a food processor, combine the flour and sugar. Add the cold butter and pulse until the mixture resembles coarse crumbs.
    - Add the egg yolk and pulse until the dough starts to come together. If needed, add cold water a tablespoon at a time until the dough holds together.
    - Form the dough into a disk, wrap it in plastic wrap, and refrigerate for at least 30 minutes.
2. **Blind Bake the Pastry:**
    - Preheat your oven to 375°F (190°C). Grease and flour a 9-inch (23cm) tart pan or line it with parchment paper.
    - Roll out the dough on a lightly floured surface to fit the tart pan. Press the dough into the pan and trim the edges. Prick the bottom with a fork.
    - Chill the pastry shell for an additional 15 minutes.
    - Line the pastry with parchment paper and fill with baking weights or dried beans.
    - Bake for 15 minutes. Remove the parchment and weights, and bake for another 10 minutes or until the crust is golden brown. Let it cool completely.
3. **Prepare the Chocolate Ganache:**
    - In a small saucepan, heat the heavy cream over medium heat until it begins to simmer. Do not let it boil.

- Place the chopped chocolate in a heatproof bowl. Pour the hot cream over the chocolate and let it sit for a minute to soften.
- Stir the mixture until smooth and fully combined. Add the butter and vanilla extract, if using, and stir until the butter is melted and the ganache is glossy.

4. **Assemble the Tart:**
    - Pour the chocolate ganache into the cooled tart shell and spread it evenly with a spatula.
    - Refrigerate the tart for at least 2 hours or until the ganache is set. If you're in a hurry, you can place it in the freezer for 30 minutes.

5. **Garnish and Serve:**
    - Before serving, garnish the tart with fresh berries, chocolate shavings, or a dollop of whipped cream if desired.
    - Dust with powdered sugar for a touch of elegance.

Tips:

- **Chocolate Quality:** Use high-quality chocolate for the best flavor and texture.
- **Crust:** Make sure the crust is fully cooled before adding the ganache to prevent it from melting.
- **Ganache Consistency:** If the ganache is too thick, you can gently reheat it over a double boiler and stir until smooth before pouring it into the tart shell.

Tarte au Chocolat is a luxurious dessert that highlights the rich and smooth taste of chocolate. It's perfect for any special occasion or as a sophisticated treat. Enjoy making and savoring this classic French tart!

Tarte à la Praliné

Ingredients:

For the Pastry:

- 1 1/4 cups (160g) all-purpose flour
- 1/4 cup (50g) granulated sugar
- 1/2 cup (115g) unsalted butter, cold and cut into small pieces
- 1 large egg yolk
- 1-2 tablespoons cold water (as needed)

For the Praliné Filling:

- 1/2 cup (100g) granulated sugar
- 1/2 cup (120ml) heavy cream
- 1/2 cup (120ml) milk
- 1/2 cup (100g) praliné paste (store-bought or homemade)
- 2 large eggs
- 1 tablespoon unsalted butter
- 1 teaspoon vanilla extract

For Garnish (optional):

- Whipped cream
- Caramelized nuts (e.g., almonds or hazelnuts)
- Powdered sugar

Instructions:

1. **Prepare the Pastry:**
   - In a food processor, combine the flour and sugar. Add the cold butter and pulse until the mixture resembles coarse crumbs.
   - Add the egg yolk and pulse until the dough starts to come together. If needed, add cold water a tablespoon at a time until the dough holds together.
   - Form the dough into a disk, wrap it in plastic wrap, and refrigerate for at least 30 minutes.
   - Preheat your oven to 375°F (190°C). Grease and flour a 9-inch (23cm) tart pan or line it with parchment paper.
   - Roll out the dough on a lightly floured surface to fit the tart pan. Press the dough into the pan and trim the edges. Prick the bottom with a fork.
   - Chill the pastry shell for an additional 15 minutes.
   - Line the pastry with parchment paper and fill with baking weights or dried beans.
   - Bake for 15 minutes. Remove the parchment and weights, and bake for another 10 minutes or until the crust is golden brown. Let it cool completely.
2. **Prepare the Praliné Filling:**

- In a medium saucepan, combine the sugar, heavy cream, and milk. Heat over medium heat, stirring until the sugar dissolves and the mixture is hot but not boiling.
- Remove from heat and stir in the praliné paste until smooth.
- In a separate bowl, whisk the eggs. Slowly add a little of the hot cream mixture to the eggs, whisking constantly to temper them.
- Gradually add the tempered egg mixture back into the saucepan with the remaining cream mixture, whisking continuously.
- Return the saucepan to the heat and cook over low heat, stirring constantly until the mixture thickens slightly (about 2-3 minutes). Do not let it boil.
- Remove from heat and stir in the butter and vanilla extract until fully incorporated.

3. **Assemble the Tart:**
    - Pour the praliné filling into the cooled tart shell and smooth the top with a spatula.
    - Bake at 350°F (175°C) for 20-25 minutes, or until the filling is set and slightly puffed. The center should be just slightly jiggly.
    - Allow the tart to cool completely before serving.
4. **Garnish and Serve:**
    - Before serving, garnish the tart with whipped cream, caramelized nuts, or a dusting of powdered sugar if desired.

Tips:

- **Praliné Paste:** You can buy praliné paste at specialty stores or make it at home by blending caramelized nuts with a bit of oil.
- **Consistency:** The filling should be smooth and creamy. If it appears too runny after baking, it may need more time in the oven.
- **Storage:** Store the tart in the refrigerator and consume within a few days for the best texture and flavor.

Tarte à la Praliné is a sophisticated and indulgent dessert that combines the rich flavor of praliné with a buttery tart crust. Enjoy making and savoring this delicious French treat!

Gâteau au Miel

Ingredients:

For the Cake:

- 1 1/2 cups (190g) all-purpose flour
- 1 teaspoon baking powder
- 1/2 teaspoon baking soda
- 1/4 teaspoon salt
- 1/2 cup (115g) unsalted butter, softened
- 1/2 cup (100g) granulated sugar
- 1/2 cup (150g) honey
- 2 large eggs
- 1/2 cup (120ml) milk
- 1 teaspoon vanilla extract

For the Glaze (optional):

- 1/4 cup (60ml) honey
- 1 tablespoon water
- 1 tablespoon lemon juice

For Garnish (optional):

- Sliced almonds
- Powdered sugar (for dusting)

Instructions:

1. **Prepare the Cake:**
    - Preheat your oven to 350°F (175°C). Grease and flour a 9-inch (23cm) round cake pan or line it with parchment paper.
    - In a medium bowl, whisk together the flour, baking powder, baking soda, and salt.
    - In a large bowl, beat the softened butter and granulated sugar together until light and fluffy.
    - Add the honey and beat until well combined.
    - Beat in the eggs, one at a time, mixing well after each addition. Stir in the vanilla extract.
    - Gradually add the flour mixture to the butter mixture, alternating with the milk, beginning and ending with the flour mixture. Mix until just combined.
    - Pour the batter into the prepared cake pan and smooth the top with a spatula.
2. **Bake the Cake:**
    - Bake in the preheated oven for 25-30 minutes, or until a toothpick inserted into the center comes out clean and the cake is golden brown.

- Let the cake cool in the pan for 10 minutes before transferring it to a wire rack to cool completely.
3. **Prepare the Glaze (optional):**
   - In a small saucepan, combine the honey, water, and lemon juice. Heat over low heat until the honey is melted and the mixture is smooth.
   - Brush the glaze over the cooled cake for a shiny finish, if desired.
4. **Garnish and Serve:**
   - Garnish with sliced almonds or a dusting of powdered sugar if desired.
   - Slice and serve the cake plain or with a cup of tea.

Tips:

- **Honey Quality:** Use high-quality honey for the best flavor. The type of honey will influence the cake's taste, so choose one that you enjoy.
- **Texture:** This cake is meant to be moist and slightly dense. Make sure not to overmix the batter to keep it tender.
- **Storage:** Store the cake in an airtight container at room temperature for up to 3-4 days. It can also be frozen for longer storage.

Gâteau au Miel is a simple yet flavorful cake that highlights the natural sweetness of honey. Enjoy making and savoring this classic French treat!

Tarte à l'Orange

Ingredients:

For the Pastry:

- 1 1/4 cups (160g) all-purpose flour
- 1/4 cup (50g) granulated sugar
- 1/2 cup (115g) unsalted butter, cold and cut into small pieces
- 1 large egg yolk
- 1-2 tablespoons cold water (as needed)

For the Orange Filling:

- 1 cup (240ml) fresh orange juice
- 1/2 cup (100g) granulated sugar
- 3 large eggs
- 1/4 cup (60ml) heavy cream
- 2 tablespoons all-purpose flour
- 1 tablespoon unsalted butter
- 1 teaspoon orange zest

For the Glaze (optional):

- 1/4 cup (60ml) apricot or orange jelly
- 1 tablespoon water

For Garnish (optional):

- Orange zest
- Fresh mint leaves

Instructions:

1. **Prepare the Pastry:**
    - In a food processor, combine the flour and sugar. Add the cold butter and pulse until the mixture resembles coarse crumbs.
    - Add the egg yolk and pulse until the dough starts to come together. If needed, add cold water a tablespoon at a time until the dough holds together.
    - Form the dough into a disk, wrap it in plastic wrap, and refrigerate for at least 30 minutes.
    - Preheat your oven to 375°F (190°C). Grease and flour a 9-inch (23cm) tart pan or line it with parchment paper.
    - Roll out the dough on a lightly floured surface to fit the tart pan. Press the dough into the pan and trim the edges. Prick the bottom with a fork.
    - Chill the pastry shell for an additional 15 minutes.

- Line the pastry with parchment paper and fill with baking weights or dried beans.
- Bake for 15 minutes. Remove the parchment and weights, and bake for another 10 minutes or until the crust is golden brown. Let it cool completely.

2. **Prepare the Orange Filling:**
    - In a medium saucepan, combine the orange juice and sugar. Heat over medium heat until the sugar dissolves.
    - In a bowl, whisk the eggs, heavy cream, and flour until smooth.
    - Gradually add a little of the hot orange juice mixture to the egg mixture to temper it, whisking constantly.
    - Pour the tempered egg mixture back into the saucepan with the remaining orange juice mixture.
    - Cook over medium heat, stirring constantly, until the mixture thickens slightly (about 5-7 minutes). Do not let it boil.
    - Remove from heat and stir in the butter and orange zest until the butter is melted and the mixture is smooth.

3. **Assemble the Tart:**
    - Pour the orange filling into the cooled tart shell and smooth the top with a spatula.
    - Bake the tart at 350°F (175°C) for 20-25 minutes, or until the filling is set and slightly puffed. The center should be just slightly jiggly.
    - Allow the tart to cool completely before serving.

4. **Prepare the Glaze (optional):**
    - In a small saucepan, heat the apricot or orange jelly with water until melted and smooth. Brush the glaze over the top of the tart for a shiny finish.

5. **Garnish and Serve:**
    - Garnish with additional orange zest and fresh mint leaves if desired.
    - Slice and serve the tart chilled or at room temperature.

Tips:

- **Orange Juice:** Use freshly squeezed orange juice for the best flavor.
- **Consistency:** Make sure the filling is thickened slightly before pouring it into the tart shell to ensure it sets properly.
- **Storage:** Store the tart in the refrigerator for up to 3-4 days.

Tarte à l'Orange is a bright and flavorful dessert that beautifully highlights the fresh and zesty taste of oranges. Enjoy making and savoring this refreshing French tart!

Gâteau de Crêpes

Ingredients:

For the Crêpes:

- 1 cup (125g) all-purpose flour
- 2 large eggs
- 1 cup (240ml) milk
- 2 tablespoons granulated sugar
- 1/4 teaspoon salt
- 2 tablespoons unsalted butter, melted
- 1 teaspoon vanilla extract (optional)

For the Filling:

- 1 cup (240ml) heavy cream
- 1/2 cup (120g) mascarpone cheese or cream cheese
- 1/4 cup (50g) granulated sugar
- 1 teaspoon vanilla extract
- Fresh berries (e.g., raspberries, strawberries) or fruit compote

For the Topping (optional):

- Powdered sugar
- Fresh berries or fruit slices
- Whipped cream

Instructions:

1. **Prepare the Crêpes:**
   - In a large bowl, whisk together the flour, eggs, milk, sugar, and salt until smooth. Stir in the melted butter and vanilla extract if using.
   - Let the batter rest for at least 30 minutes at room temperature.
   - Heat a non-stick skillet or crêpe pan over medium heat and lightly grease with butter or oil.
   - Pour a small amount of batter into the pan and quickly tilt and swirl to spread it evenly. Cook for about 1-2 minutes, or until the edges start to lift and the bottom is golden brown.
   - Flip the crêpe and cook for another 30 seconds to 1 minute. Transfer to a plate and repeat with the remaining batter, stacking the crêpes as you go. Allow them to cool completely.
2. **Prepare the Filling:**
   - In a large bowl, beat the heavy cream until stiff peaks form.
   - Gently fold in the mascarpone cheese, granulated sugar, and vanilla extract until well combined and smooth.

3. **Assemble the Gâteau de Crêpes:**
    - Place one crêpe on a serving plate. Spread a thin layer of the cream filling over the crêpe.
    - Add a few fresh berries or a spoonful of fruit compote on top of the cream, if using.
    - Place another crêpe on top and repeat the process, layering crêpes, cream filling, and fruit until all the crêpes are used.
    - Finish with a final layer of cream filling on top.
4. **Garnish and Serve:**
    - Garnish the top with fresh berries, fruit slices, and a dusting of powdered sugar if desired.
    - Serve the Gâteau de Crêpes immediately, or chill it in the refrigerator for an hour or so to allow the flavors to meld.

Tips:

- **Crêpe Texture:** Ensure the crêpes are fully cooled before assembling the cake to prevent the filling from melting or making the crêpes soggy.
- **Filling Variations:** You can use other fillings such as lemon curd, chocolate ganache, or pastry cream for different flavors.
- **Fruit Compote:** If using fruit compote, ensure it's not too watery to avoid soggy crêpes.

Gâteau de Crêpes is a versatile and elegant dessert that showcases the delicate nature of crêpes and can be customized with your favorite flavors and fillings. Enjoy making and indulging in this delicious French treat!

Gâteau au Fromage Blanc

Ingredients:

For the Crust:

- 1 1/2 cups (150g) graham cracker crumbs or crushed digestive biscuits
- 1/4 cup (50g) granulated sugar
- 1/2 cup (115g) unsalted butter, melted

For the Filling:

- 2 cups (500g) fromage blanc (or substitute with ricotta or quark)
- 3 large eggs
- 1 cup (200g) granulated sugar
- 1 teaspoon vanilla extract
- 1/2 cup (120ml) sour cream or heavy cream
- 1 tablespoon all-purpose flour
- Zest of 1 lemon (optional)

For the Topping (optional):

- Fresh fruit (e.g., berries, sliced peaches)
- Fruit compote or sauce
- Powdered sugar for dusting

Instructions:

1. **Prepare the Crust:**
   - Preheat your oven to 350°F (175°C).
   - In a medium bowl, combine the graham cracker crumbs, granulated sugar, and melted butter. Mix until the crumbs are evenly coated and the mixture resembles wet sand.
   - Press the mixture into the bottom of a 9-inch (23cm) springform pan to form an even layer. Use the back of a spoon to press it down firmly.
   - Bake the crust for about 10 minutes or until it's lightly golden. Remove from the oven and let it cool.
2. **Prepare the Filling:**
   - In a large bowl, whisk together the fromage blanc, eggs, granulated sugar, and vanilla extract until smooth and well combined.
   - Stir in the sour cream or heavy cream, flour, and lemon zest (if using) until the mixture is smooth.
   - Pour the filling over the cooled crust in the springform pan.
3. **Bake the Cake:**

- Bake the gâteau au fromage blanc in the preheated oven for 45-50 minutes, or until the center is set and the edges are slightly puffed. The center may still be a bit jiggly but should firm up as it cools.
- Turn off the oven and let the cake cool in the oven with the door slightly ajar for about 1 hour to prevent cracking.
- Remove the cake from the oven and refrigerate for at least 4 hours or overnight to allow it to set completely.

4. **Garnish and Serve:**
   - Before serving, garnish the top with fresh fruit, fruit compote, or a dusting of powdered sugar if desired.
   - Run a knife around the edge of the cake before removing the sides of the springform pan.

Tips:

- **For a Smooth Texture:** Ensure that all ingredients are at room temperature before mixing to avoid lumps.
- **Prevent Cracking:** Let the cake cool gradually in the oven with the door slightly open to prevent it from cracking.
- **Flavor Variations:** You can add different flavorings such as vanilla bean, almond extract, or citrus zest to the filling for a unique twist.

Gâteau au Fromage Blanc is a light and creamy dessert that's perfect for any occasion. Its delicate flavor and smooth texture make it a sophisticated and enjoyable treat. Enjoy making and savoring this classic French dessert!

Tarte aux Poireaux

Ingredients:

For the Pastry:

- 1 1/4 cups (160g) all-purpose flour
- 1/4 teaspoon salt
- 1/2 cup (115g) unsalted butter, cold and cut into small pieces
- 1 large egg yolk
- 1-2 tablespoons cold water (as needed)

For the Filling:

- 3-4 medium leeks (about 1 pound or 450g)
- 2 tablespoons olive oil
- 1/2 cup (120ml) heavy cream
- 1/2 cup (120ml) milk
- 3 large eggs
- 1 cup (100g) grated Gruyère cheese or other cheese of your choice
- 1/2 teaspoon dried thyme or 1 teaspoon fresh thyme leaves
- Salt and freshly ground black pepper to taste

For Garnish (optional):

- Fresh herbs (e.g., thyme or parsley)
- Extra cheese for sprinkling

Instructions:

1. **Prepare the Pastry:**
   - In a food processor, combine the flour and salt. Add the cold butter and pulse until the mixture resembles coarse crumbs.
   - Add the egg yolk and pulse until the dough starts to come together. If needed, add cold water a tablespoon at a time until the dough holds together.
   - Form the dough into a disk, wrap it in plastic wrap, and refrigerate for at least 30 minutes.
   - Preheat your oven to 375°F (190°C). Grease and flour a 9-inch (23cm) tart pan or line it with parchment paper.
   - Roll out the dough on a lightly floured surface to fit the tart pan. Press the dough into the pan and trim the edges. Prick the bottom with a fork.
   - Chill the pastry shell for an additional 15 minutes.
   - Line the pastry with parchment paper and fill with baking weights or dried beans.
   - Bake for 15 minutes. Remove the parchment and weights, and bake for another 10 minutes or until the crust is golden brown. Let it cool slightly.
2. **Prepare the Filling:**

- While the pastry is baking, clean the leeks thoroughly, removing the dark green parts and slicing the remaining white and light green parts into thin rings.
- In a large skillet, heat the olive oil over medium heat. Add the leeks and cook, stirring occasionally, until softened and lightly caramelized, about 10 minutes. Season with a pinch of salt and pepper.
- In a bowl, whisk together the heavy cream, milk, and eggs until well combined. Stir in the grated cheese, thyme, and additional salt and pepper.
- Spread the cooked leeks evenly over the partially baked tart crust.

3. **Assemble and Bake:**
   - Pour the cream mixture over the leeks in the tart shell.
   - Bake in the preheated oven for 30-35 minutes, or until the filling is set and the top is golden brown.
   - Allow the tart to cool slightly before serving. Garnish with fresh herbs and extra cheese if desired.

4. **Serve:**
   - Serve warm or at room temperature. The tart pairs well with a green salad or as part of a larger meal.

Tips:

- **Leek Preparation:** Ensure that the leeks are cleaned thoroughly to remove any grit or sand. Slice them thinly for even cooking.
- **Cheese:** Gruyère cheese adds a nice nutty flavor, but you can use other cheeses like cheddar, Swiss, or a mix.
- **Storage:** Store any leftover tart in the refrigerator for up to 3 days. Reheat in the oven or enjoy cold.

Tarte aux Poireaux is a flavorful and comforting dish that highlights the delicate taste of leeks. Enjoy making and savoring this classic French savory tart!

Tarte aux Pêches

Ingredients:

For the Pastry:

- 1 1/4 cups (160g) all-purpose flour
- 1/4 cup (50g) granulated sugar
- 1/2 cup (115g) unsalted butter, cold and cut into small pieces
- 1 large egg yolk
- 1-2 tablespoons cold water (as needed)

For the Filling:

- 4-5 ripe peaches (about 4 cups sliced, peeled, and pitted)
- 1/4 cup (50g) granulated sugar (adjust based on peach sweetness)
- 1 tablespoon cornstarch
- 1 teaspoon vanilla extract
- 1/2 teaspoon ground cinnamon (optional)
- Juice of 1/2 lemon
- 1 egg, beaten (for egg wash)

For the Glaze (optional):

- 1/4 cup (60ml) apricot or peach jam
- 1 tablespoon water

For Garnish (optional):

- Fresh mint leaves
- Powdered sugar for dusting

Instructions:

1. **Prepare the Pastry:**
   - In a food processor, combine the flour and sugar. Add the cold butter and pulse until the mixture resembles coarse crumbs.
   - Add the egg yolk and pulse until the dough starts to come together. If needed, add cold water a tablespoon at a time until the dough holds together.
   - Form the dough into a disk, wrap it in plastic wrap, and refrigerate for at least 30 minutes.
   - Preheat your oven to 375°F (190°C). Grease and flour a 9-inch (23cm) tart pan or line it with parchment paper.
   - Roll out the dough on a lightly floured surface to fit the tart pan. Press the dough into the pan and trim the edges. Prick the bottom with a fork.
   - Chill the pastry shell for an additional 15 minutes.

- Line the pastry with parchment paper and fill with baking weights or dried beans.
- Bake for 15 minutes. Remove the parchment and weights, and bake for another 10 minutes or until the crust is golden brown. Let it cool slightly.

2. **Prepare the Peach Filling:**
   - Peel and pit the peaches, then slice them into thin wedges.
   - In a bowl, toss the peach slices with granulated sugar, cornstarch, vanilla extract, ground cinnamon (if using), and lemon juice. The cornstarch will help thicken the filling as it bakes.

3. **Assemble the Tart:**
   - Arrange the peach slices in the partially baked tart shell in a decorative pattern, overlapping them slightly.
   - Brush the edges of the pastry with the beaten egg to give it a golden finish.
   - Bake the tart in the preheated oven for 30-35 minutes, or until the peaches are tender and the crust is golden brown.

4. **Prepare the Glaze (optional):**
   - While the tart is baking, combine the apricot or peach jam with water in a small saucepan over low heat. Stir until melted and smooth.
   - Brush the glaze over the baked tart while it is still warm for a shiny finish.

5. **Garnish and Serve:**
   - Let the tart cool slightly before removing it from the tart pan.
   - Garnish with fresh mint leaves and a dusting of powdered sugar if desired.
   - Serve warm or at room temperature.

Tips:

- **Peach Ripeness:** Use ripe but firm peaches for the best texture and flavor. Overripe peaches may become too mushy during baking.
- **Glaze:** The glaze helps to give the tart a beautiful shine and adds a touch of sweetness. If you prefer a less sweet tart, you can skip the glaze.
- **Storage:** Store any leftover tart in the refrigerator for up to 3 days. It can be enjoyed cold or at room temperature.

Tarte aux Pêches is a delightful and summery dessert that highlights the natural sweetness and flavor of fresh peaches. Enjoy making and savoring this classic French tart!

Gâteau au Praliné

Ingredients:

For the Praliné Paste:

- 1 cup (120g) hazelnuts (or almonds)
- 1/2 cup (100g) granulated sugar
- 1/4 cup (60ml) water

For the Cake:

- 1 1/2 cups (190g) all-purpose flour
- 1 1/2 teaspoons baking powder
- 1/2 teaspoon salt
- 1/2 cup (115g) unsalted butter, softened
- 1 cup (200g) granulated sugar
- 3 large eggs
- 1/2 cup (120ml) milk
- 1/2 cup (120ml) praliné paste (store-bought or homemade)

For the Praliné Cream Filling:

- 1 cup (240ml) heavy cream
- 1/2 cup (120ml) praliné paste
- 1 tablespoon powdered sugar

For the Ganache (optional):

- 1/2 cup (120ml) heavy cream
- 4 ounces (115g) dark chocolate, chopped
- 2 tablespoons unsalted butter

For Garnish (optional):

- Chopped hazelnuts
- Caramel shards

Instructions:

1. **Prepare the Praliné Paste:**
   - Preheat your oven to 350°F (175°C). Spread the hazelnuts on a baking sheet and toast in the oven for about 10 minutes, or until the skins are darkened and the nuts are fragrant. Allow to cool slightly.
   - Place the toasted nuts in a clean kitchen towel and rub them to remove the skins.

- In a small saucepan, combine the sugar and water. Heat over medium heat until the sugar dissolves and the mixture turns a golden amber color.
- Carefully stir in the toasted nuts and continue cooking for another 2-3 minutes, until the nuts are well coated and the caramel is thickened.
- Pour the caramelized nuts onto a parchment-lined baking sheet and let cool completely.
- Once cool, break into pieces and process in a food processor until it forms a smooth paste. This is your praliné paste.

2. **Prepare the Cake:**
    - Preheat your oven to 350°F (175°C). Grease and flour two 8-inch (20cm) round cake pans or line them with parchment paper.
    - In a medium bowl, whisk together the flour, baking powder, and salt.
    - In a large bowl, beat the softened butter and granulated sugar until light and fluffy.
    - Add the eggs one at a time, beating well after each addition. Mix in the praliné paste until well combined.
    - Gradually add the flour mixture to the butter mixture, alternating with the milk, beginning and ending with the flour mixture. Mix until just combined.
    - Divide the batter evenly between the prepared pans and smooth the tops.
    - Bake for 25-30 minutes, or until a toothpick inserted into the center comes out clean and the cakes are golden brown.
    - Allow the cakes to cool in the pans for 10 minutes before transferring them to a wire rack to cool completely.

3. **Prepare the Praliné Cream Filling:**
    - In a large bowl, beat the heavy cream with an electric mixer until stiff peaks form.
    - Fold in the praliné paste and powdered sugar until well combined.

4. **Prepare the Ganache (optional):**
    - In a small saucepan, heat the heavy cream until just simmering.
    - Pour the hot cream over the chopped chocolate in a heatproof bowl. Let it sit for 1-2 minutes, then stir until smooth.
    - Stir in the butter until fully incorporated.

5. **Assemble the Cake:**
    - Place one cake layer on a serving plate. Spread half of the praliné cream filling over the top.
    - Place the second cake layer on top and spread the remaining praliné cream filling over the top and sides of the cake.
    - If using ganache, pour it over the top of the cake, letting it drip down the sides. Alternatively, spread the ganache evenly over the cake.

6. **Garnish and Serve:**
    - Garnish with chopped hazelnuts and caramel shards if desired.
    - Allow the cake to set for at least an hour before serving to let the flavors meld.

Tips:

- **Praliné Paste:** You can buy praliné paste from specialty stores or online if you prefer not to make it yourself.
- **Flavor Variations:** You can add a splash of liqueur, such as Frangelico or Amaretto, to the cake batter or filling for an extra layer of flavor.
- **Storage:** Store the cake in an airtight container at room temperature for up to 3 days or in the refrigerator for up to a week.

Gâteau au Praliné is a rich and decadent dessert that beautifully showcases the nutty, caramelized flavor of praliné. Enjoy making and indulging in this luxurious French treat!

Madeleines au Citron

Ingredients:

For the Madeleines:

- 1/2 cup (115g) unsalted butter, plus extra for greasing the pan
- 1 cup (120g) all-purpose flour
- 1 teaspoon baking powder
- 1/4 teaspoon salt
- 1/2 cup (100g) granulated sugar
- 2 large eggs
- Zest of 1 lemon
- 2 tablespoons freshly squeezed lemon juice
- 1 teaspoon vanilla extract (optional)

For the Glaze (optional):

- 1/2 cup (60g) powdered sugar
- 1-2 tablespoons freshly squeezed lemon juice

Instructions:

1. **Prepare the Batter:**
    - Preheat your oven to 375°F (190°C). Grease a madeleine pan with butter and lightly flour it, or use a non-stick madeleine pan.
    - Melt the 1/2 cup of butter in a small saucepan or microwave, then let it cool slightly.
    - In a medium bowl, whisk together the flour, baking powder, and salt.
    - In a large bowl, beat the granulated sugar and eggs with an electric mixer until the mixture is pale and thick, about 2-3 minutes.
    - Add the lemon zest, lemon juice, and vanilla extract (if using) to the egg mixture. Mix to combine.
    - Gradually fold in the flour mixture until just combined.
    - Gently fold in the melted butter until fully incorporated, being careful not to overmix.
2. **Fill the Pan:**
    - Spoon the batter into the prepared madeleine pan, filling each mold about 3/4 full. You can use a small cookie scoop or a spoon to do this.
    - For a nice hump, chill the filled madeleine pan in the refrigerator for 10-15 minutes before baking.
3. **Bake the Madeleines:**
    - Bake in the preheated oven for 10-12 minutes, or until the edges are golden brown and the centers are set.

- Remove the madeleines from the oven and let them cool in the pan for about 5 minutes before transferring them to a wire rack to cool completely.
4. **Prepare the Glaze (optional):**
    - While the madeleines are cooling, mix the powdered sugar with 1-2 tablespoons of lemon juice until you have a smooth, pourable glaze.
    - Drizzle the glaze over the cooled madeleines or dip the tops into the glaze.
5. **Serve:**
    - Serve the madeleines as a sweet treat with tea or coffee. They are best enjoyed fresh but can be stored in an airtight container for up to 3 days.

Tips:

- **Butter Temperature:** Make sure the melted butter is slightly cooled before adding it to the batter to avoid curdling the eggs.
- **Pan:** Use a proper madeleine pan for the classic shell shape, but if you don't have one, you can use a mini muffin pan as an alternative.
- **Chilling:** Chilling the batter-filled pan before baking helps achieve the classic madeleine "hump."

Madeleines au Citron are a delightful combination of tender crumb and zesty lemon flavor, perfect for a light and elegant treat. Enjoy baking and savoring these charming French cakes!

Tarte aux Noix

Ingredients:

For the Pastry:

- 1 1/4 cups (160g) all-purpose flour
- 1/4 cup (50g) granulated sugar
- 1/2 cup (115g) unsalted butter, cold and cut into small pieces
- 1 large egg yolk
- 1-2 tablespoons cold water (as needed)

For the Filling:

- 1 cup (120g) walnuts, roughly chopped
- 1/2 cup (100g) granulated sugar
- 1/4 cup (50g) packed light brown sugar
- 1/2 cup (120ml) heavy cream
- 1/4 cup (60ml) honey
- 3 large eggs
- 1 teaspoon vanilla extract
- A pinch of salt

For Garnish (optional):

- Whole walnut halves
- Powdered sugar for dusting

Instructions:

1. **Prepare the Pastry:**
   - In a food processor, combine the flour and granulated sugar. Add the cold butter and pulse until the mixture resembles coarse crumbs.
   - Add the egg yolk and pulse until the dough starts to come together. If needed, add cold water a tablespoon at a time until the dough holds together.
   - Form the dough into a disk, wrap it in plastic wrap, and refrigerate for at least 30 minutes.
   - Preheat your oven to 375°F (190°C). Grease and flour a 9-inch (23cm) tart pan or line it with parchment paper.
   - Roll out the dough on a lightly floured surface to fit the tart pan. Press the dough into the pan and trim the edges. Prick the bottom with a fork.
   - Chill the pastry shell for an additional 15 minutes.
   - Line the pastry with parchment paper and fill with baking weights or dried beans.
   - Bake for 15 minutes. Remove the parchment and weights, and bake for another 10 minutes or until the crust is golden brown. Let it cool slightly.
2. **Prepare the Filling:**

- In a large bowl, whisk together the granulated sugar, brown sugar, heavy cream, honey, eggs, vanilla extract, and a pinch of salt until well combined.
- Stir in the chopped walnuts until evenly distributed.

3. **Assemble and Bake:**
   - Pour the nut filling into the partially baked tart shell and spread it out evenly.
   - Garnish with whole walnut halves if desired.
   - Bake in the preheated oven for 25-30 minutes, or until the filling is set and the top is golden brown. The filling should be slightly puffed but not liquid.

4. **Cool and Serve:**
   - Allow the tart to cool completely before removing it from the tart pan.
   - Dust with powdered sugar if desired before serving.

Tips:

- **Nuts:** You can use other nuts such as pecans or almonds if you prefer. Adjust the size of the nuts in the filling if using larger or smaller varieties.
- **Glaze:** For extra shine, you can brush the top of the tart with a bit of warmed apricot jam or honey after baking.
- **Storage:** Store the tart in an airtight container at room temperature for up to 3 days or refrigerate for up to a week.

Tarte aux Noix is a rich and indulgent dessert that combines a buttery crust with a sweet and nutty filling. It's perfect for special occasions or as a treat for yourself. Enjoy baking and savoring this classic French tart!

Cannelés

Ingredients:

For the Batter:

- 2 cups (500ml) whole milk
- 1/2 cup (100g) granulated sugar
- 1/2 cup (100g) all-purpose flour
- 2 large eggs
- 1 large egg yolk
- 2 tablespoons unsalted butter
- 2 tablespoons dark rum
- 1 vanilla bean (or 1 tablespoon vanilla extract)

For the Molds:

- 2 tablespoons unsalted butter, melted (for greasing the molds)
- 1 tablespoon all-purpose flour (for dusting the molds)

Instructions:

1. **Prepare the Batter:**
   - **Vanilla Bean:** If using a vanilla bean, split it lengthwise and scrape out the seeds. Add both the seeds and the pod to the milk. Heat the milk in a saucepan until it just begins to simmer. Remove from heat and let it infuse for 10 minutes. If using vanilla extract, skip this step and add the extract later.
   - In a separate bowl, whisk together the eggs, egg yolk, and granulated sugar until light and frothy.
   - Remove the vanilla bean pod from the milk and discard it. Stir in the butter until melted.
   - Gradually add the milk mixture to the egg mixture, whisking continuously to combine.
   - Sift the flour and gradually add it to the mixture, whisking until smooth and lump-free.
   - Stir in the rum. Let the batter sit in the refrigerator for at least 24 hours, but up to 48 hours for best results. This resting period helps develop the flavor and texture.
2. **Prepare the Molds:**
   - Preheat your oven to 450°F (230°C).
   - Brush the cannelé molds generously with melted butter, making sure to coat the sides thoroughly. Dust with flour, tapping out any excess. This helps create the crispy, caramelized crust.
3. **Bake the Cannelés:**
   - Fill each mold about 3/4 full with the chilled batter. The batter will rise a bit during baking.

- Place the molds on a baking sheet for easy handling. Bake in the preheated oven for 10 minutes at 450°F (230°C).
- Reduce the temperature to 375°F (190°C) and bake for an additional 45-50 minutes, or until the cannelés are deeply caramelized and have a firm crust. They should be dark brown on the outside and soft on the inside.

4. **Cool and Serve:**
    - Remove the cannelés from the oven and let them cool in the molds for about 10 minutes.
    - Gently unmold the cannelés by tapping them on the counter or using a small knife if needed.
    - Serve warm or at room temperature. They are best enjoyed fresh but can be stored in an airtight container for up to 3 days.

Tips:

- **Molds:** Traditional cannelé molds are made of copper, but silicone or non-stick molds can also be used. Copper molds help achieve the classic crispy crust.
- **Batter Resting:** The longer you let the batter rest, the better the cannelés will be. If you don't have 24 hours, try to rest it for at least a few hours.
- **Overbaking:** Cannelés should be dark brown but not burnt. Keep an eye on them during the final baking stage to avoid overbaking.

Cannelés are a delicious and unique French pastry that pairs beautifully with coffee or tea. Their caramelized exterior and soft, flavorful interior make them a special treat that's well worth the effort. Enjoy baking and savoring these delightful pastries!

Tarte au Fromage

Ingredients:

For the Pastry:

- 1 1/4 cups (160g) all-purpose flour
- 1/4 teaspoon salt
- 1/2 cup (115g) unsalted butter, cold and cut into small pieces
- 1 large egg yolk
- 1-2 tablespoons cold water (as needed)

For the Cheese Filling:

- 1 cup (240ml) heavy cream
- 1 cup (240ml) milk
- 3 large eggs
- 1 cup (100g) grated Gruyère cheese (or another cheese of your choice, such as cheddar or Swiss)
- 1/2 cup (50g) crumbled feta cheese (optional)
- 1/4 cup (30g) grated Parmesan cheese (optional)
- 1 tablespoon chopped fresh herbs (such as thyme, chives, or parsley)
- Salt and freshly ground black pepper to taste

For Garnish (optional):

- Fresh herbs
- Extra grated cheese

Instructions:

1. **Prepare the Pastry:**
    - In a food processor, combine the flour and salt. Add the cold butter and pulse until the mixture resembles coarse crumbs.
    - Add the egg yolk and pulse until the dough starts to come together. If needed, add cold water a tablespoon at a time until the dough holds together.
    - Form the dough into a disk, wrap it in plastic wrap, and refrigerate for at least 30 minutes.
    - Preheat your oven to 375°F (190°C). Grease and flour a 9-inch (23cm) tart pan or line it with parchment paper.
    - Roll out the dough on a lightly floured surface to fit the tart pan. Press the dough into the pan and trim the edges. Prick the bottom with a fork.
    - Chill the pastry shell for an additional 15 minutes.
    - Line the pastry with parchment paper and fill with baking weights or dried beans.
    - Bake for 15 minutes. Remove the parchment and weights, and bake for another 10 minutes or until the crust is golden brown. Let it cool slightly.

2. **Prepare the Cheese Filling:**
   - In a large bowl, whisk together the heavy cream, milk, and eggs until well combined.
   - Stir in the grated Gruyère cheese, crumbled feta cheese (if using), grated Parmesan cheese (if using), and chopped fresh herbs.
   - Season the mixture with salt and freshly ground black pepper to taste.
3. **Assemble and Bake:**
   - Pour the cheese filling into the partially baked tart shell and spread it out evenly.
   - Bake in the preheated oven for 25-30 minutes, or until the filling is set and the top is golden brown.
4. **Cool and Serve:**
   - Allow the tart to cool slightly before removing it from the pan.
   - Garnish with fresh herbs and extra cheese if desired.
   - Serve warm or at room temperature. This tart pairs well with a simple green salad or can be served as part of a larger meal.

Tips:

- **Cheese Varieties:** Feel free to experiment with different cheeses or combinations to suit your taste. Other good options include goat cheese, blue cheese, or a mix of cheeses.
- **Add-Ins:** You can add vegetables like sautéed mushrooms, spinach, or caramelized onions to the filling for extra flavor and texture.
- **Storage:** Store any leftover tart in the refrigerator for up to 3 days. It can be reheated in the oven or enjoyed cold.

Tarte au Fromage is a versatile and delicious savory tart that's easy to make and perfect for any meal. Enjoy baking and savoring this classic French dish!

Gâteau à la Vanille

Ingredients:

For the Cake:

- 1 1/2 cups (190g) all-purpose flour
- 1 1/2 teaspoons baking powder
- 1/4 teaspoon salt
- 1/2 cup (115g) unsalted butter, softened
- 1 cup (200g) granulated sugar
- 2 large eggs
- 1 cup (240ml) whole milk
- 1 tablespoon vanilla extract
- 1 teaspoon vanilla bean paste (optional, for extra vanilla flavor)

For the Vanilla Glaze (optional):

- 1 cup (120g) powdered sugar
- 2 tablespoons whole milk
- 1/2 teaspoon vanilla extract

For Garnish (optional):

- Fresh berries
- Whipped cream
- Powdered sugar

Instructions:

1. **Prepare the Cake:**
   - Preheat your oven to 350°F (175°C). Grease and flour an 8-inch (20cm) round cake pan or line it with parchment paper.
   - In a medium bowl, whisk together the flour, baking powder, and salt.
   - In a large bowl, beat the softened butter and granulated sugar with an electric mixer until light and fluffy, about 3-4 minutes.
   - Add the eggs one at a time, beating well after each addition. Mix in the vanilla extract and vanilla bean paste (if using).
   - Gradually add the dry ingredients to the butter mixture, alternating with the milk, beginning and ending with the flour mixture. Mix until just combined.
   - Pour the batter into the prepared cake pan and smooth the top.
2. **Bake the Cake:**
   - Bake in the preheated oven for 25-30 minutes, or until a toothpick inserted into the center comes out clean and the top is golden brown.
   - Allow the cake to cool in the pan for 10 minutes before transferring it to a wire rack to cool completely.

3. **Prepare the Vanilla Glaze (optional):**
    - In a small bowl, whisk together the powdered sugar, milk, and vanilla extract until smooth and pourable.
    - Drizzle the glaze over the cooled cake.
4. **Garnish and Serve:**
    - Garnish the cake with fresh berries, whipped cream, or a dusting of powdered sugar if desired.
    - Slice and serve. The cake can be enjoyed on its own or with a variety of toppings.

Tips:

- **Cake Variations:** You can add lemon zest or other flavorings to the batter if you want to experiment with different flavors.
- **Layer Cake:** If you want to make a layered cake, you can double the recipe and bake it in two 8-inch (20cm) round pans, then layer and frost as desired.
- **Storage:** Store the cake in an airtight container at room temperature for up to 3 days, or in the refrigerator for up to a week.

Gâteau à la Vanille is a timeless and versatile vanilla cake that is sure to please any palate. Enjoy baking and savoring this classic French treat!

Tarte aux Mûres

Ingredients:

For the Pastry:

- 1 1/4 cups (160g) all-purpose flour
- 1/4 cup (50g) granulated sugar
- 1/2 cup (115g) unsalted butter, cold and cut into small pieces
- 1 large egg yolk
- 1-2 tablespoons cold water (as needed)

For the Blackberry Filling:

- 2 cups (300g) fresh blackberries (or thawed frozen blackberries)
- 1/2 cup (100g) granulated sugar
- 2 tablespoons cornstarch
- 1 tablespoon lemon juice
- 1 teaspoon vanilla extract
- 1/4 teaspoon salt

For the Topping (optional):

- 1 tablespoon granulated sugar (for sprinkling)
- Fresh blackberries for garnish
- Powdered sugar for dusting

Instructions:

1. **Prepare the Pastry:**
   - In a food processor, combine the flour and granulated sugar. Add the cold butter and pulse until the mixture resembles coarse crumbs.
   - Add the egg yolk and pulse until the dough starts to come together. If needed, add cold water a tablespoon at a time until the dough holds together.
   - Form the dough into a disk, wrap it in plastic wrap, and refrigerate for at least 30 minutes.
   - Preheat your oven to 375°F (190°C). Grease and flour a 9-inch (23cm) tart pan or line it with parchment paper.
   - Roll out the dough on a lightly floured surface to fit the tart pan. Press the dough into the pan and trim the edges. Prick the bottom with a fork.
   - Chill the pastry shell for an additional 15 minutes.
   - Line the pastry with parchment paper and fill with baking weights or dried beans.
   - Bake for 15 minutes. Remove the parchment and weights, and bake for another 10 minutes or until the crust is golden brown. Let it cool slightly.
2. **Prepare the Blackberry Filling:**

- In a medium saucepan, combine the blackberries, granulated sugar, cornstarch, lemon juice, vanilla extract, and salt. Cook over medium heat, stirring frequently, until the mixture begins to thicken and bubble, about 5-7 minutes.
- Remove from heat and let the filling cool slightly before pouring it into the partially baked tart shell.

3. **Assemble and Bake:**
    - Pour the blackberry filling into the partially baked tart shell and spread it evenly.
    - If desired, sprinkle the top with granulated sugar for a bit of extra sweetness and a slight crunch.
    - Bake in the preheated oven for 20-25 minutes, or until the filling is set and the top is slightly bubbly.
4. **Cool and Serve:**
    - Allow the tart to cool completely before removing it from the pan.
    - Garnish with fresh blackberries and a dusting of powdered sugar if desired.

Tips:

- **Berry Variations:** You can substitute blackberries with other berries like raspberries, blueberries, or a mixed berry blend if you prefer.
- **Pastry Options:** If you prefer, you can use a store-bought tart shell or pie dough to save time.
- **Storage:** Store the tart in an airtight container at room temperature for up to 3 days, or in the refrigerator for up to a week.

Tarte aux Mûres is a delightful dessert that highlights the natural sweetness and tartness of blackberries. Enjoy making and savoring this classic French tart!

Tarte au Caramel

Ingredients:

For the Pastry:

- 1 1/4 cups (160g) all-purpose flour
- 1/4 cup (50g) granulated sugar
- 1/2 cup (115g) unsalted butter, cold and cut into small pieces
- 1 large egg yolk
- 1-2 tablespoons cold water (as needed)

For the Caramel Filling:

- 1 cup (200g) granulated sugar
- 6 tablespoons unsalted butter, cut into pieces
- 1/2 cup (120ml) heavy cream
- 1/4 cup (60ml) light corn syrup (or golden syrup)
- 1/4 teaspoon salt
- 1 teaspoon vanilla extract

For the Garnish (optional):

- Sea salt flakes
- Whipped cream

Instructions:

1. **Prepare the Pastry:**
    - In a food processor, combine the flour and granulated sugar. Add the cold butter and pulse until the mixture resembles coarse crumbs.
    - Add the egg yolk and pulse until the dough starts to come together. If needed, add cold water a tablespoon at a time until the dough holds together.
    - Form the dough into a disk, wrap it in plastic wrap, and refrigerate for at least 30 minutes.
    - Preheat your oven to 375°F (190°C). Grease and flour a 9-inch (23cm) tart pan or line it with parchment paper.
    - Roll out the dough on a lightly floured surface to fit the tart pan. Press the dough into the pan and trim the edges. Prick the bottom with a fork.
    - Chill the pastry shell for an additional 15 minutes.
    - Line the pastry with parchment paper and fill with baking weights or dried beans.
    - Bake for 15 minutes. Remove the parchment and weights, and bake for another 10 minutes or until the crust is golden brown. Let it cool completely.
2. **Prepare the Caramel Filling:**

- In a medium saucepan, combine the granulated sugar and corn syrup over medium heat. Cook, stirring occasionally, until the sugar dissolves and the mixture begins to boil.
- Continue cooking without stirring until the caramel reaches a deep amber color. Be careful not to let it burn.
- Remove the saucepan from heat and carefully add the butter, stirring until melted and smooth.
- Slowly add the heavy cream while continuing to stir (the mixture will bubble up). Stir in the salt and vanilla extract.
- Let the caramel cool slightly before pouring it into the cooled tart shell.

3. **Assemble and Chill:**
   - Pour the caramel filling into the cooled tart shell and spread it out evenly.
   - Let the tart cool to room temperature, then refrigerate for at least 2 hours, or until the caramel is set.

4. **Garnish and Serve:**
   - Before serving, sprinkle sea salt flakes on top of the caramel if desired.
   - Serve with a dollop of whipped cream or enjoy on its own.

Tips:

- **Caramel Consistency:** Be careful not to overcook the caramel, as it can become too hard once it cools. It should be smooth and pourable when you add it to the tart shell.
- **Make Ahead:** The tart can be made a day or two in advance. Store it in the refrigerator until ready to serve.
- **Presentation:** For a decorative touch, you can drizzle extra caramel sauce over the top or around the plate when serving.

Tarte au Caramel is a rich and indulgent dessert that is sure to impress with its smooth caramel filling and buttery crust. Enjoy making and savoring this decadent treat!

Gâteau au Café

Ingredients:

For the Cake:

- 1 1/2 cups (190g) all-purpose flour
- 1 1/2 teaspoons baking powder
- 1/4 teaspoon salt
- 1/2 cup (115g) unsalted butter, softened
- 1 cup (200g) granulated sugar
- 2 large eggs
- 1/2 cup (120ml) strong brewed coffee, cooled
- 1/4 cup (60ml) milk
- 1 teaspoon vanilla extract
- 1 tablespoon instant coffee granules or espresso powder (optional, for extra coffee flavor)

For the Coffee Glaze (optional):

- 1/2 cup (60g) powdered sugar
- 1 tablespoon brewed coffee
- 1/2 teaspoon vanilla extract

For Garnish (optional):

- Whipped cream
- Chocolate shavings

Instructions:

1. **Prepare the Cake:**
    - Preheat your oven to 350°F (175°C). Grease and flour an 8-inch (20cm) round cake pan or line it with parchment paper.
    - In a medium bowl, whisk together the flour, baking powder, and salt.
    - In a large bowl, beat the softened butter and granulated sugar with an electric mixer until light and fluffy, about 3-4 minutes.
    - Add the eggs one at a time, beating well after each addition. Mix in the vanilla extract.
    - Gradually add the dry ingredients to the butter mixture, alternating with the brewed coffee and milk, beginning and ending with the flour mixture. Mix until just combined. If using instant coffee granules or espresso powder, dissolve them in the coffee before adding.
    - Pour the batter into the prepared cake pan and smooth the top.
2. **Bake the Cake:**

- Bake in the preheated oven for 25-30 minutes, or until a toothpick inserted into the center comes out clean and the top is golden brown.
- Allow the cake to cool in the pan for 10 minutes before transferring it to a wire rack to cool completely.
3. **Prepare the Coffee Glaze (optional):**
    - In a small bowl, whisk together the powdered sugar, brewed coffee, and vanilla extract until smooth and pourable.
    - Drizzle the glaze over the cooled cake.
4. **Garnish and Serve:**
    - Garnish with whipped cream and chocolate shavings if desired.
    - Serve the cake at room temperature. It pairs wonderfully with a cup of coffee or tea.

Tips:

- **Coffee Strength:** Use strong brewed coffee for a more pronounced coffee flavor. You can also adjust the amount of instant coffee or espresso powder to taste.
- **Make Ahead:** The cake can be made a day in advance. Store it in an airtight container at room temperature or in the refrigerator.
- **Variations:** You can add a layer of coffee-flavored frosting or fill the cake with a coffee-flavored mousse for extra indulgence.

Gâteau au Café is a delightful coffee-flavored cake that's both simple and elegant. Enjoy baking and savoring this treat with your favorite coffee or tea!

Tarte au Pralin

Ingredients:

For the Pastry:

- 1 1/4 cups (160g) all-purpose flour
- 1/4 cup (50g) granulated sugar
- 1/2 cup (115g) unsalted butter, cold and cut into small pieces
- 1 large egg yolk
- 1-2 tablespoons cold water (as needed)

For the Praline Filling:

- 1 cup (200g) granulated sugar
- 1/2 cup (120ml) water
- 1 cup (100g) hazelnuts, toasted and skinless
- 1/2 cup (120ml) heavy cream
- 1/4 cup (60g) unsalted butter, at room temperature
- 1/4 cup (60ml) milk
- 1 teaspoon vanilla extract
- Pinch of salt

For Garnish (optional):

- Crushed hazelnuts
- Whipped cream

Instructions:

1. **Prepare the Pastry:**
    - In a food processor, combine the flour and granulated sugar. Add the cold butter and pulse until the mixture resembles coarse crumbs.
    - Add the egg yolk and pulse until the dough starts to come together. If needed, add cold water a tablespoon at a time until the dough holds together.
    - Form the dough into a disk, wrap it in plastic wrap, and refrigerate for at least 30 minutes.
    - Preheat your oven to 375°F (190°C). Grease and flour a 9-inch (23cm) tart pan or line it with parchment paper.
    - Roll out the dough on a lightly floured surface to fit the tart pan. Press the dough into the pan and trim the edges. Prick the bottom with a fork.
    - Chill the pastry shell for an additional 15 minutes.
    - Line the pastry with parchment paper and fill with baking weights or dried beans.
    - Bake for 15 minutes. Remove the parchment and weights, and bake for another 10 minutes or until the crust is golden brown. Let it cool completely.
2. **Prepare the Praline Filling:**

- **Make the Praline:** In a medium saucepan, combine the granulated sugar and water over medium heat. Cook, stirring occasionally, until the sugar dissolves and the mixture begins to simmer. Continue cooking without stirring until the syrup turns a deep amber color.
- Remove from heat and carefully stir in the toasted hazelnuts. Pour the mixture onto a parchment-lined baking sheet and let it cool and harden.
- Once cooled, break the praline into pieces and blend in a food processor until it becomes a smooth paste.
- **Prepare the Filling:** In a separate saucepan, heat the heavy cream until just simmering. Remove from heat and whisk in the butter until melted and smooth.
- Stir in the praline paste, milk, vanilla extract, and a pinch of salt until well combined.

3. **Assemble the Tart:**
   - Pour the praline filling into the cooled tart shell and spread it out evenly.
   - Refrigerate for at least 2 hours, or until the filling is set.
4. **Garnish and Serve:**
   - Garnish with crushed hazelnuts and a dollop of whipped cream if desired.
   - Serve chilled or at room temperature.

Tips:

- **Hazelnuts:** To toast hazelnuts, spread them on a baking sheet and bake at 350°F (175°C) for 10-12 minutes, or until fragrant. Rub them in a clean kitchen towel to remove the skins.
- **Storage:** The tart can be stored in the refrigerator for up to a week. It can also be frozen for up to 3 months; thaw it in the refrigerator before serving.

Tarte au Pralin is a rich and indulgent dessert that highlights the sweet and nutty flavors of praline. Enjoy making and savoring this elegant French treat!

Tarte au Chocolat et aux Noix

Ingredients:

For the Pastry:

- 1 1/4 cups (160g) all-purpose flour
- 1/4 cup (50g) granulated sugar
- 1/2 cup (115g) unsalted butter, cold and cut into small pieces
- 1 large egg yolk
- 1-2 tablespoons cold water (as needed)

For the Chocolate Filling:

- 1 cup (240ml) heavy cream
- 8 ounces (225g) bittersweet or semisweet chocolate, chopped
- 2 large eggs
- 1 teaspoon vanilla extract

For the Nut Topping:

- 1/2 cup (60g) chopped nuts (such as walnuts, pecans, or almonds)
- 2 tablespoons granulated sugar
- 1 tablespoon unsalted butter, melted

Instructions:

1. **Prepare the Pastry:**
    - In a food processor, combine the flour and granulated sugar. Add the cold butter and pulse until the mixture resembles coarse crumbs.
    - Add the egg yolk and pulse until the dough starts to come together. If needed, add cold water a tablespoon at a time until the dough holds together.
    - Form the dough into a disk, wrap it in plastic wrap, and refrigerate for at least 30 minutes.
    - Preheat your oven to 375°F (190°C). Grease and flour a 9-inch (23cm) tart pan or line it with parchment paper.
    - Roll out the dough on a lightly floured surface to fit the tart pan. Press the dough into the pan and trim the edges. Prick the bottom with a fork.
    - Chill the pastry shell for an additional 15 minutes.
    - Line the pastry with parchment paper and fill with baking weights or dried beans.
    - Bake for 15 minutes. Remove the parchment and weights, and bake for another 10 minutes or until the crust is golden brown. Let it cool completely.
2. **Prepare the Chocolate Filling:**
    - In a medium saucepan, heat the heavy cream over medium heat until just simmering.

- Remove from heat and add the chopped chocolate, stirring until smooth and melted.
- Whisk in the eggs and vanilla extract until well combined.
3. **Assemble and Bake:**
    - Pour the chocolate filling into the cooled tart shell and smooth the top.
    - In a small bowl, toss the chopped nuts with granulated sugar and melted butter. Sprinkle the nut mixture evenly over the chocolate filling.
    - Bake in the preheated oven for 15-20 minutes, or until the filling is set and the nuts are golden brown.
4. **Cool and Serve:**
    - Allow the tart to cool to room temperature before removing it from the pan.
    - Serve as is or with a dollop of whipped cream.

Tips:

- **Chocolate Selection:** Use high-quality chocolate for the best flavor. Bittersweet or semisweet chocolate works well, but you can use milk chocolate for a sweeter filling.
- **Nut Variations:** Feel free to use your favorite nuts or a mix of nuts for the topping.
- **Storage:** Store the tart in an airtight container at room temperature for up to 3 days or in the refrigerator for up to a week. It can also be frozen for up to 2 months; thaw in the refrigerator before serving.

Tarte au Chocolat et aux Noix is a rich and satisfying dessert that pairs the smoothness of chocolate with the crunch of nuts. Enjoy making and indulging in this elegant French tart!

Tarte au Crumble

Ingredients:

For the Pastry:

- 1 1/4 cups (160g) all-purpose flour
- 1/4 cup (50g) granulated sugar
- 1/2 cup (115g) unsalted butter, cold and cut into small pieces
- 1 large egg yolk
- 1-2 tablespoons cold water (as needed)

For the Filling:

- 3 cups (about 450g) fresh fruit (such as apples, berries, or a combination)
- 1/4 cup (50g) granulated sugar
- 1 tablespoon all-purpose flour
- 1 teaspoon lemon juice
- 1/2 teaspoon vanilla extract

For the Crumble Topping:

- 1/2 cup (65g) all-purpose flour
- 1/2 cup (100g) granulated sugar
- 1/2 cup (115g) unsalted butter, cold and cut into small pieces
- 1/4 teaspoon ground cinnamon (optional)
- 1/4 cup (25g) rolled oats (optional, for extra texture)

Instructions:

1. **Prepare the Pastry:**
    - In a food processor, combine the flour and granulated sugar. Add the cold butter and pulse until the mixture resembles coarse crumbs.
    - Add the egg yolk and pulse until the dough starts to come together. If needed, add cold water a tablespoon at a time until the dough holds together.
    - Form the dough into a disk, wrap it in plastic wrap, and refrigerate for at least 30 minutes.
    - Preheat your oven to 375°F (190°C). Grease and flour a 9-inch (23cm) tart pan or line it with parchment paper.
    - Roll out the dough on a lightly floured surface to fit the tart pan. Press the dough into the pan and trim the edges. Prick the bottom with a fork.
    - Chill the pastry shell for an additional 15 minutes.
    - Line the pastry with parchment paper and fill with baking weights or dried beans.
    - Bake for 15 minutes. Remove the parchment and weights, and bake for another 10 minutes or until the crust is golden brown. Let it cool completely.
2. **Prepare the Filling:**

- Peel and core the apples if using, then cut them into thin slices. For berries, simply wash and pat them dry.
- In a large bowl, combine the fruit with granulated sugar, flour, lemon juice, and vanilla extract. Toss until the fruit is well coated.

3. **Prepare the Crumble Topping:**
   - In a medium bowl, combine the flour, sugar, and optional cinnamon. Add the cold butter and use your fingers or a pastry cutter to blend until the mixture resembles coarse crumbs. If using oats, stir them in.
4. **Assemble and Bake:**
   - Pour the fruit filling into the cooled tart shell and spread it out evenly.
   - Sprinkle the crumble topping evenly over the fruit.
   - Bake in the preheated oven for 30-35 minutes, or until the topping is golden brown and the fruit is bubbling.
5. **Cool and Serve:**
   - Allow the tart to cool for a bit before slicing. Serve warm or at room temperature, optionally with a dollop of whipped cream or a scoop of vanilla ice cream.

Tips:

- **Fruit Variations:** You can use other fruits such as pears, peaches, or plums. Adjust the sugar in the filling according to the sweetness of the fruit.
- **Make Ahead:** The tart can be made a day in advance and stored at room temperature. Reheat in a low oven if desired before serving.
- **Texture:** For a crunchier topping, add more oats or use brown sugar instead of granulated sugar.

Tarte au Crumble is a comforting dessert that brings together the tender, flavorful fruit and a crispy, buttery topping. Enjoy making and indulging in this classic French treat!

Gâteau au Pêches et au Miel

Ingredients:

For the Cake:

- 1 1/2 cups (190g) all-purpose flour
- 1 1/2 teaspoons baking powder
- 1/4 teaspoon salt
- 1/2 cup (115g) unsalted butter, softened
- 1/2 cup (100g) granulated sugar
- 1/4 cup (60g) honey
- 2 large eggs
- 1/2 cup (120ml) milk
- 1 teaspoon vanilla extract
- 2 cups (300g) fresh peaches, peeled and sliced (or use canned or frozen peaches, thawed and drained)

For the Glaze (optional):

- 2 tablespoons honey
- 1 tablespoon water

Instructions:

1. **Prepare the Cake Batter:**
    - Preheat your oven to 350°F (175°C). Grease and flour an 8-inch (20cm) round cake pan or line it with parchment paper.
    - In a medium bowl, whisk together the flour, baking powder, and salt.
    - In a large bowl, beat the softened butter and granulated sugar with an electric mixer until light and fluffy, about 3-4 minutes.
    - Add the honey and beat until well combined.
    - Add the eggs one at a time, beating well after each addition. Mix in the vanilla extract.
    - Gradually add the dry ingredients to the butter mixture, alternating with the milk, beginning and ending with the flour mixture. Mix until just combined.
    - Gently fold in the sliced peaches.
2. **Bake the Cake:**
    - Pour the batter into the prepared cake pan and spread it out evenly.
    - Bake in the preheated oven for 35-40 minutes, or until a toothpick inserted into the center comes out clean and the top is golden brown.
    - Allow the cake to cool in the pan for 10 minutes, then transfer to a wire rack to cool completely.
3. **Prepare the Glaze (optional):**

- In a small saucepan, combine the honey and water. Heat over low heat, stirring until the honey is dissolved and the mixture is smooth.
- Brush the glaze over the cooled cake for a shiny finish and added sweetness.
4. **Serve:**
    - Slice and serve the cake at room temperature. It pairs well with a dollop of whipped cream or a scoop of vanilla ice cream if desired.

Tips:

- **Peach Preparation:** If using fresh peaches, make sure they are ripe for the best flavor. Peel and slice them thinly for even distribution in the cake.
- **Flavor Variations:** For added flavor, you can sprinkle some cinnamon or nutmeg into the batter or add a teaspoon of lemon zest.
- **Make Ahead:** The cake can be made a day in advance and stored at room temperature or in the refrigerator. Reheat slightly if desired before serving.

Gâteau aux Pêches et au Miel is a sweet and comforting cake that beautifully highlights the flavors of peaches and honey. Enjoy this delightful dessert with your family and friends!

Tarte aux Amandes

Ingredients:

For the Pastry:

- 1 1/4 cups (160g) all-purpose flour
- 1/4 cup (50g) granulated sugar
- 1/2 cup (115g) unsalted butter, cold and cut into small pieces
- 1 large egg yolk
- 1-2 tablespoons cold water (as needed)

For the Almond Filling:

- 1/2 cup (115g) unsalted butter, softened
- 1/2 cup (100g) granulated sugar
- 1/2 cup (50g) almond flour (or ground almonds)
- 2 large eggs
- 1 teaspoon vanilla extract
- 2 tablespoons all-purpose flour
- 1/4 teaspoon almond extract (optional, for extra almond flavor)

For the Garnish:

- 1/4 cup (25g) slivered almonds
- Powdered sugar, for dusting (optional)

Instructions:

1. **Prepare the Pastry:**
    - In a food processor, combine the flour and granulated sugar. Add the cold butter and pulse until the mixture resembles coarse crumbs.
    - Add the egg yolk and pulse until the dough starts to come together. If needed, add cold water a tablespoon at a time until the dough holds together.
    - Form the dough into a disk, wrap it in plastic wrap, and refrigerate for at least 30 minutes.
    - Preheat your oven to 375°F (190°C). Grease and flour a 9-inch (23cm) tart pan or line it with parchment paper.
    - Roll out the dough on a lightly floured surface to fit the tart pan. Press the dough into the pan and trim the edges. Prick the bottom with a fork.
    - Chill the pastry shell for an additional 15 minutes.
    - Line the pastry with parchment paper and fill with baking weights or dried beans.
    - Bake for 15 minutes. Remove the parchment and weights, and bake for another 10 minutes or until the crust is golden brown. Let it cool completely.
2. **Prepare the Almond Filling:**

- In a large bowl, beat the softened butter and granulated sugar until light and fluffy.
- Add the almond flour and mix until well combined.
- Beat in the eggs one at a time, mixing well after each addition.
- Stir in the vanilla extract, flour, and almond extract (if using) until smooth.

3. **Assemble and Bake:**
    - Pour the almond filling into the cooled tart shell and spread it out evenly.
    - Sprinkle the slivered almonds over the top of the filling.
    - Bake in the preheated oven for 25-30 minutes, or until the filling is set and lightly golden brown.
4. **Cool and Serve:**
    - Allow the tart to cool completely before removing it from the pan.
    - Dust with powdered sugar if desired before serving.

Tips:

- **Almond Flour:** Make sure the almond flour is finely ground for a smooth filling. You can also grind whole almonds if needed.
- **Flavor Variations:** You can add a bit of lemon zest or a splash of amaretto to the filling for additional flavor.
- **Storage:** The tart can be stored at room temperature for up to 3 days or in the refrigerator for up to a week. It can also be frozen for up to 2 months; thaw in the refrigerator before serving.

Tarte aux Amandes is a delightful and sophisticated dessert that pairs beautifully with a cup of tea or coffee. Enjoy making and savoring this French classic!

Tarte aux Abricots

Ingredients:

For the Pastry:

- 1 1/4 cups (160g) all-purpose flour
- 1/4 cup (50g) granulated sugar
- 1/2 cup (115g) unsalted butter, cold and cut into small pieces
- 1 large egg yolk
- 1-2 tablespoons cold water (as needed)

For the Apricot Filling:

- 1 pound (450g) fresh apricots, pitted and halved
- 1/4 cup (50g) granulated sugar
- 1 tablespoon lemon juice
- 1 tablespoon all-purpose flour

For the Almond Cream (optional but recommended):

- 1/2 cup (115g) unsalted butter, softened
- 1/2 cup (100g) granulated sugar
- 1/2 cup (50g) almond flour (or ground almonds)
- 2 large eggs
- 1 teaspoon vanilla extract
- 1 tablespoon all-purpose flour

For the Glaze (optional):

- 2 tablespoons apricot jam
- 1 tablespoon water

Instructions:

1. **Prepare the Pastry:**
    - In a food processor, combine the flour and granulated sugar. Add the cold butter and pulse until the mixture resembles coarse crumbs.
    - Add the egg yolk and pulse until the dough starts to come together. If needed, add cold water a tablespoon at a time until the dough holds together.
    - Form the dough into a disk, wrap it in plastic wrap, and refrigerate for at least 30 minutes.
    - Preheat your oven to 375°F (190°C). Grease and flour a 9-inch (23cm) tart pan or line it with parchment paper.
    - Roll out the dough on a lightly floured surface to fit the tart pan. Press the dough into the pan and trim the edges. Prick the bottom with a fork.

- Chill the pastry shell for an additional 15 minutes.
- Line the pastry with parchment paper and fill with baking weights or dried beans.
- Bake for 15 minutes. Remove the parchment and weights, and bake for another 10 minutes or until the crust is golden brown. Let it cool completely.

2. **Prepare the Apricot Filling:**
    - In a bowl, toss the apricot halves with sugar, lemon juice, and flour. Set aside.
3. **Prepare the Almond Cream (if using):**
    - In a medium bowl, beat the softened butter and granulated sugar until light and fluffy.
    - Add the almond flour and mix until well combined.
    - Beat in the eggs one at a time, mixing well after each addition.
    - Stir in the vanilla extract and flour until smooth.
4. **Assemble the Tart:**
    - If using almond cream, spread a thin layer of almond cream over the bottom of the cooled tart shell.
    - Arrange the apricot halves, cut side up, over the almond cream or directly on the tart shell if not using almond cream.
    - Bake in the preheated oven for 25-30 minutes, or until the apricots are tender and the almond cream or tart shell is golden brown.
5. **Prepare the Glaze (optional):**
    - In a small saucepan, heat the apricot jam and water over low heat until smooth and melted.
    - Brush the glaze over the apricots to give them a shiny finish.
6. **Cool and Serve:**
    - Allow the tart to cool completely before removing it from the pan.
    - Serve at room temperature or chilled. It's delicious on its own or with a dollop of whipped cream or a scoop of vanilla ice cream.

Tips:

- **Apricot Ripeness:** Use ripe but firm apricots for the best flavor and texture. If apricots are not in season, you can use canned apricots, but make sure they are well-drained.
- **Almond Cream:** The almond cream adds a rich, nutty flavor and a creamy texture, but you can omit it for a simpler tart if preferred.
- **Storage:** The tart can be stored at room temperature for up to 2 days or in the refrigerator for up to a week. It can also be frozen for up to 2 months; thaw in the refrigerator before serving.

Tarte aux Abricots is a delicious and elegant dessert that beautifully showcases the natural sweetness of apricots. Enjoy making and savoring this French classic!

Gâteau de Voyage

Ingredients:

For the Cake:

- 1 1/2 cups (190g) all-purpose flour
- 1 cup (200g) granulated sugar
- 1/2 cup (115g) unsalted butter, softened
- 3 large eggs
- 1/2 cup (120ml) milk
- 1 teaspoon vanilla extract
- 1 1/2 teaspoons baking powder
- 1/4 teaspoon salt
- Zest of 1 lemon or orange (optional, for added flavor)

For the Glaze (optional):

- 1/2 cup (60g) powdered sugar
- 2 tablespoons lemon juice or milk

Instructions:

1. **Prepare the Cake Batter:**
    - Preheat your oven to 350°F (175°C). Grease and flour a loaf pan (8x4 inches or 9x5 inches) or line it with parchment paper.
    - In a medium bowl, whisk together the flour, baking powder, and salt.
    - In a large bowl, cream together the softened butter and granulated sugar until light and fluffy.
    - Beat in the eggs one at a time, mixing well after each addition. Stir in the vanilla extract and lemon or orange zest if using.
    - Gradually add the dry ingredients to the butter mixture, alternating with the milk, beginning and ending with the flour mixture. Mix until just combined.
2. **Bake the Cake:**
    - Pour the batter into the prepared loaf pan and smooth the top with a spatula.
    - Bake in the preheated oven for 50-60 minutes, or until a toothpick inserted into the center comes out clean and the top is golden brown.
    - Allow the cake to cool in the pan for 10 minutes, then transfer to a wire rack to cool completely.
3. **Prepare the Glaze (optional):**
    - In a small bowl, whisk together the powdered sugar and lemon juice or milk until smooth.
    - Drizzle the glaze over the cooled cake for a sweet finish.
4. **Serve:**

- Slice and serve the cake at room temperature. It's perfect for a snack, with coffee or tea, or as a simple dessert.

Tips:

- **Flavor Variations:** You can add mix-ins like chocolate chips, nuts, or dried fruits to the batter for extra texture and flavor.
- **Storage:** The cake keeps well at room temperature for up to a week. It can also be wrapped tightly and frozen for up to 2 months; thaw in the refrigerator before serving.
- **For Travel:** If you're making this cake for travel, it's sturdy enough to hold up well over time and can be enjoyed without refrigeration.

Gâteau de Voyage is a versatile and enduring recipe that's perfect for enjoying on the go or savoring at home. Its simple ingredients and rich flavor make it a favorite in French baking tradition.

Gâteau à la Crème de Marron

Ingredients:

For the Cake:

- 1 cup (125g) all-purpose flour
- 1/2 cup (100g) granulated sugar
- 1/2 cup (115g) unsalted butter, softened
- 1/2 cup (125g) crème de marron (chestnut cream)
- 2 large eggs
- 1 teaspoon baking powder
- 1/4 teaspoon salt
- 1/2 teaspoon vanilla extract

For the Chestnut Cream Filling:

- 1/2 cup (125g) crème de marron (chestnut cream)
- 1/2 cup (120ml) heavy cream

For the Glaze (optional):

- 1/2 cup (125g) crème de marron (chestnut cream)
- 2 tablespoons heavy cream

Instructions:

1. **Prepare the Cake Batter:**
    - Preheat your oven to 350°F (175°C). Grease and flour an 8-inch (20cm) round cake pan or line it with parchment paper.
    - In a medium bowl, whisk together the flour, baking powder, and salt.
    - In a large bowl, cream together the softened butter and granulated sugar until light and fluffy.
    - Beat in the eggs one at a time, mixing well after each addition. Stir in the vanilla extract and crème de marron until combined.
    - Gradually add the dry ingredients to the butter mixture, mixing until just combined.
2. **Bake the Cake:**
    - Pour the batter into the prepared cake pan and smooth the top with a spatula.
    - Bake in the preheated oven for 25-30 minutes, or until a toothpick inserted into the center comes out clean and the cake is golden brown.
    - Allow the cake to cool in the pan for 10 minutes, then transfer to a wire rack to cool completely.
3. **Prepare the Chestnut Cream Filling:**
    - In a medium bowl, whip the heavy cream until stiff peaks form.
    - Gently fold the crème de marron into the whipped cream until well combined.

4. **Assemble the Cake:**
   - Once the cake is completely cooled, slice it in half horizontally to create two layers.
   - Spread the chestnut cream filling evenly over the bottom layer of the cake.
   - Place the second layer on top.
5. **Prepare the Glaze (optional):**
   - In a small bowl, whisk together the crème de marron and heavy cream until smooth.
   - Spread or drizzle the glaze over the top of the cake.
6. **Serve:**
   - Slice and serve the cake at room temperature. It pairs well with a cup of tea or coffee.

Tips:

- **Crème de Marron:** Crème de marron can be found in specialty stores or online. If you can't find it, you can make your own by blending cooked chestnuts with sugar and a bit of water until smooth.
- **Storage:** The cake can be stored in an airtight container at room temperature for up to 3 days, or in the refrigerator for up to a week. It can also be frozen for up to 2 months; thaw in the refrigerator before serving.
- **Flavor Variations:** Add a touch of cinnamon or a splash of vanilla extract to the filling for additional flavor.

Gâteau à la Crème de Marron is a rich and elegant dessert that highlights the unique flavor of chestnuts. Enjoy making and savoring this French classic!

Tarte aux Raisins

Ingredients:

For the Pastry:

- 1 1/4 cups (160g) all-purpose flour
- 1/4 cup (50g) granulated sugar
- 1/2 cup (115g) unsalted butter, cold and cut into small pieces
- 1 large egg yolk
- 1-2 tablespoons cold water (as needed)

For the Custard Filling:

- 1 cup (240ml) milk
- 1/2 cup (100g) granulated sugar
- 3 large egg yolks
- 2 tablespoons all-purpose flour
- 1/4 teaspoon vanilla extract
- 1 tablespoon unsalted butter

For the Topping:

- 2 cups (300g) fresh grapes (red or green, or a mix), washed and halved
- 1/4 cup (50g) granulated sugar (optional, for sprinkling)

For the Glaze (optional):

- 2 tablespoons apricot jam
- 1 tablespoon water

Instructions:

1. **Prepare the Pastry:**
    - In a food processor, combine the flour and granulated sugar. Add the cold butter and pulse until the mixture resembles coarse crumbs.
    - Add the egg yolk and pulse until the dough starts to come together. If needed, add cold water a tablespoon at a time until the dough holds together.
    - Form the dough into a disk, wrap it in plastic wrap, and refrigerate for at least 30 minutes.
    - Preheat your oven to 375°F (190°C). Grease and flour a 9-inch (23cm) tart pan or line it with parchment paper.
    - Roll out the dough on a lightly floured surface to fit the tart pan. Press the dough into the pan and trim the edges. Prick the bottom with a fork.
    - Chill the pastry shell for an additional 15 minutes.
    - Line the pastry with parchment paper and fill with baking weights or dried beans.

- Bake for 15 minutes. Remove the parchment and weights, and bake for another 10 minutes or until the crust is golden brown. Let it cool completely.
2. **Prepare the Custard Filling:**
    - In a medium saucepan, heat the milk over medium heat until it begins to simmer. Remove from heat.
    - In a bowl, whisk together the egg yolks and granulated sugar until pale and thick. Add the flour and whisk until smooth.
    - Gradually pour the hot milk into the egg mixture, whisking constantly to prevent curdling.
    - Return the mixture to the saucepan and cook over medium heat, whisking constantly, until the custard thickens and just begins to boil.
    - Remove from heat and stir in the vanilla extract and butter until smooth. Let the custard cool slightly.
3. **Assemble the Tart:**
    - Spread the custard filling evenly over the cooled pastry shell.
    - Arrange the halved grapes evenly over the custard.
4. **Prepare the Glaze (optional):**
    - In a small saucepan, heat the apricot jam and water over low heat until smooth and melted.
    - Brush the glaze over the grapes to give them a shiny finish.
5. **Serve:**
    - Allow the tart to cool completely before serving.
    - Serve at room temperature or chilled.

Tips:

- **Grape Preparation:** If you prefer, you can remove the grape skins before adding them to the tart. Simply blanch the grapes in boiling water for a few seconds, then transfer them to an ice bath and peel off the skins.
- **Flavor Variations:** For added flavor, you can sprinkle a bit of cinnamon or nutmeg over the custard before adding the grapes.
- **Storage:** The tart can be stored in an airtight container in the refrigerator for up to 3 days. It is best enjoyed within a day or two of making.

Tarte aux Raisins is a fresh and elegant dessert that beautifully highlights the natural sweetness of grapes. Enjoy making and savoring this classic French treat!

Tarte au Miel et aux Amandes

Ingredients:

For the Pastry:

- 1 1/4 cups (160g) all-purpose flour
- 1/4 cup (50g) granulated sugar
- 1/2 cup (115g) unsalted butter, cold and cut into small pieces
- 1 large egg yolk
- 1-2 tablespoons cold water (as needed)

For the Almond Cream Filling:

- 1/2 cup (115g) unsalted butter, softened
- 1/2 cup (100g) granulated sugar
- 1/2 cup (50g) almond flour (or ground almonds)
- 2 large eggs
- 1 teaspoon vanilla extract
- 1 tablespoon all-purpose flour

For the Honey Glaze:

- 1/4 cup (60ml) honey
- 2 tablespoons heavy cream

For Garnish:

- 1/4 cup (25g) slivered almonds

Instructions:

1. **Prepare the Pastry:**
    - In a food processor, combine the flour and granulated sugar. Add the cold butter and pulse until the mixture resembles coarse crumbs.
    - Add the egg yolk and pulse until the dough starts to come together. If needed, add cold water a tablespoon at a time until the dough holds together.
    - Form the dough into a disk, wrap it in plastic wrap, and refrigerate for at least 30 minutes.
    - Preheat your oven to 375°F (190°C). Grease and flour a 9-inch (23cm) tart pan or line it with parchment paper.
    - Roll out the dough on a lightly floured surface to fit the tart pan. Press the dough into the pan and trim the edges. Prick the bottom with a fork.
    - Chill the pastry shell for an additional 15 minutes.
    - Line the pastry with parchment paper and fill with baking weights or dried beans.

- Bake for 15 minutes. Remove the parchment and weights, and bake for another 10 minutes or until the crust is golden brown. Let it cool completely.

2. **Prepare the Almond Cream Filling:**
   - In a large bowl, beat the softened butter and granulated sugar until light and fluffy.
   - Add the almond flour and mix until well combined.
   - Beat in the eggs one at a time, mixing well after each addition.
   - Stir in the vanilla extract and flour until smooth.

3. **Assemble the Tart:**
   - Spread the almond cream filling evenly over the cooled pastry shell.
   - Bake in the preheated oven for 25-30 minutes, or until the filling is set and lightly golden brown.
   - Remove from the oven and allow to cool slightly.

4. **Prepare the Honey Glaze:**
   - In a small saucepan, combine the honey and heavy cream. Heat over low heat, stirring until the mixture is smooth and combined.
   - Brush the honey glaze over the warm tart.

5. **Add the Garnish:**
   - Sprinkle the slivered almonds over the glazed tart.

6. **Cool and Serve:**
   - Allow the tart to cool completely before serving. It can be served at room temperature or slightly warm.

Tips:

- **Almond Flour:** For a finer texture, use blanched almond flour. You can also make your own by processing whole almonds until finely ground.
- **Honey Glaze:** If the glaze becomes too thick, you can warm it gently to make it easier to brush over the tart.
- **Storage:** The tart can be stored in an airtight container at room temperature for up to 3 days. It can also be refrigerated for up to a week or frozen for up to 2 months; thaw in the refrigerator before serving.

Tarte au Miel et aux Amandes is a sweet and nutty dessert that is perfect for special occasions or as a treat to enjoy with a cup of tea or coffee. Enjoy making and savoring this classic French tart!